WAR IS A RACKET

T0105325

Photo courtesy of the Butler family.

Smedley Butler with the USMC mascot bulldogs at an Army-Navy game.

WAR IS A RACKET

The Antiwar Classic by
America's Most Decorated Soldier

**Brigadier General
Smedley Darlington Butler**

Foreword by
David Talbot

Introduction by
Jesse Ventura

Afterword by
Cindy Sheehan

SKYHORSE PUBLISHING

Additional material copyright © 2013, 2016 by Skyhorse Publishing, Inc.
Introduction copyright © 2013 by Jesse Ventura
Foreword copyright © 2016 by David Talbot
Afterword copyright © 2016 by Cindy Sheehan
Photographs and radio address courtesy of the Butler Family
Other materials courtesy of the Marine Corps Archives & Special Collections

No claim is made to material contained in this work that is derived from
government documents. Nevertheless, Skyhorse Publishing claims copyright in all
additional content, including, but not limited to, compilation copyright and the
copyright in and to any additional material, elements, design, images, or layout
of whatever kind included herein.

All inquiries should be addressed to Skyhorse Publishing, 307 West
36th Street, 11th Floor, New York, NY 10018.

Skyhorse Publishing books may be purchased in bulk at special discounts for
sales promotion, corporate gifts, fund-raising, or educational purposes. Special
editions can also be created to specifications. For details, contact the Special Sales
Department, Skyhorse Publishing, 307 West 36th Street,
11th Floor, New York, NY 10018 or info@skyhorsepublishing.com.

Skyhorse® and Skyhorse Publishing® are registered trademarks of
Skyhorse Publishing, Inc.®, a Delaware corporation.

Visit our website at www.skyhorsepublishing.com.

10 9 8 7 6 5 4

Cover design by Rain Saukas
Cover photo: iStockphoto

Library of Congress Cataloging-in-Publication Data is available on file.

ISBN: 978-1-5107-0427-5
Ebook ISBN: 978-1-5107-0428-2

Printed in the United States of America

Butler with his wife, Ethel Conway Peters Butler, circa 1901.

Butler with his son, Smedley Butler Jr.

Photos courtesy of the Butler family.

Photo courtesy of the Butler family.

Butler at home with his cat.

Contents

BUTLER, CIVIC AND MILITARY LEADER

Maj. Gen. Smedley Darlington Butler was born in Pennsylvania of an old Quaker family. He lives at Newtown Square, Del. Co. His father, the late Congressman Thomas S. Butler, of West Chester, was long a leader of the House of Representatives.

Gen. Butler is one of the only four Americans ever awarded two Congressional Medals of Honor.

Gen. Butler entered the Marine Corps when sixteen years old. He served in the Spanish-American War, in Cuba, in the Philippines, in China during the Boxer Rebellion, in many South American countries, in Mexico, in France during the World War, and finally in China in 1927, where the situation was so serious that he was sent with 5,000 Marines. They left in 1929, however, without firing a shot. Gen. Butler's diplomacy ended the trouble and won high praise from the Chinese.

In the World War he commanded the embarkation camp at Brest, the greatest camp of its kind in the history of the world. He found it a sink of mud and disease. His handling of it won a citation from Gen. Pershing, who said: "Confronted with problems of extraordinary magnitude in supervising the reception, entertainment and departure of the large number of officers and soldiers passing through this camp, he has solved all with conspicuous success, performing services of the highest character for the American Expeditionary Forces."

1,800,000 men passed through that camp while he was in command. For his work at Brest he received Distinguished Service Medals from both the Army and Navy.

Gen. Butler has been under fire in defense of the American flag more than 120 times.

In 1924, when crime had gone beyond control, Gen. Butler was drafted by the Mayor of Philadelphia to be Director of Public Safety. He reorganized the police, drove out or jailed the criminal element, and cleaned up the City. His work was so effective that the Vare machine had him fired.

Gen. Butler is not only a most distinguished fighter, but a great administrator and diplomat. President Roosevelt said of him: "Smedley Butler is the ideal American soldier."

ELECT THIS FIGHTER
U. S. SENATOR

SMEDLEY D. BUTLER

We need a man in Washington who cannot be bought, bluffed, or bullied, who stands for the plain people, and does not shift his ground for any boss.

REPUBLICAN CANDIDATE
PRIMARY ELECTION, APRIL 26

Issued by the Independent Republican State Committee Widener Building 4 Philadelphia, Pa.

BUTLER'S PLEDGES TO THE PEOPLE

If elected U. S. Senator, I will use the whole power of my office in support of these principles:

Millions of men, women and children are facing starvation, through no fault of their own. No red-blooded American can forget them. Every worker has the right to work. The duty of the Federal Government is to see that he gets work. We can borrow money enough to build roads and other public works, give our people jobs, restore their buying power, drive the depression away, and pay it back when good times return.

Pennsylvania's basic industries—farming, manufacturing, and mining—have been stifled and handicapped long enough. I promise my support to every measure which offers work to every Pennsylvanian who digs under the ground, grows anything in the ground, builds anything on the ground, or manufactures anything.

Pennsylvania needs, and I will demand, real tariff protection. Many foreign products from countries which keep our goods out are today underselling our own products in our own markets. We are false to the interest of our workers if we allow this.

I am a dry. The 18th Amendment as part of the Constitution is the supreme law of the land. Now, as always, I stand squarely on the Constitution. The paramount issue today is not whether Pennsylvanians shall drink but whether they shall eat.

I believe in the right of labor to organize, bargain collectively, and protect its own interest, and I will support it in doing so.

I am for strict limitation of immigration, but members of families of those already here should be admitted. The foreigner who becomes a good citizen is entitled to our help and respect, but racketeers who violate our laws should be deported.

The Nation and the progressive States should provide for maintaining the American standard of living, and for old age pensions. I am for both.

Public utilities affect our lives for good or evil every day. In the interest of their shareholders, as well as the general public, they must be brought under effective government control and regulation.

The investing public and depositors in banks must be protected. I pledge myself to help do so.

I believe in taxing prosperity and not adversity, and in postponing new taxation until prosperity comes back. Those who profit most under our government should pay most to maintain it.

I am for Federal aid for main roads and back roads, thus reducing taxes on farmers and home owners.

Government expenditures can and must be reduced, but not those which give work to the needy.

I am opposed to war except in defense. The way to keep out of war is to play square, maintain an adequate Navy, and be properly prepared.

I believe in disarmament on the basis of rifle for rifle, gun for gun, and ship for ship.

I am opposed to sending American boys to be killed abroad in defense of the investments of international bankers.

I am opposed to laying the burden of Europe's debts on the backs of our people. It is time for the American government to give its attention to its own people at home.

The men who fought the World War are entitled to the best this Nation can give them. Those who came through and the dependents of those who died are entitled to proper bonuses and pensions. And the poor fellows who are maimed or mentally wrecked should be given the finest care. I have always been one of them and I always will be.

Smedley D. Butler

Flier courtesy of the Butler family.

An election flier from an unsuccessful run at U.S. Senator in 1932.

Editor's Note

Major General Smedley D. Butler was an American hero. His knowledge and teachings not only improved our military, but our country as a whole.

With special thanks to Molly Swanton and the Butler family, as well as Christopher Ellis at the Marine Corps Archives & Special Collections, we have been able to not only publish Major General Butler's famous exposé, *War Is a Racket*, but several other essays, articles, and speeches.

While we have transcribed several of these works, we wanted to include some of them in their original format. Because of this, there may be marks or other comments on the documents. We at Skyhorse felt that showing the truest and most authentic form of General Butler's works would be best in remembering and respecting one of the most decorated Marines in United States history.

We hope that you enjoy his work as much as we have and that you'll gain much wisdom and insight from "The Old Gimlet."

Foreword

By David Talbot

Boys dream of war. That's how I began *Devil Dog*, my illustrated biography of Smedley Darlington Butler, the legendary Marine hero. Butler ran off to join the Marines at the tender age of sixteen in 1898, just as the American empire began its rise. He made his military debut in Cuba during the Spanish American War—and then proceeded to follow America's bloody imperial path around the world. Like many young men of his time—and today—Butler thought of war as a glorious, flag-waving adventure. "As a youngster, I loved the excitement of battle," he said late in his life. "It's lots of fun, you know, and it's nice to strut around in front of your wife—or somebody else's wife—and display your medals and your uniform.

"But there's another side to it," Butler bleakly added, making it clear that he had seen all too much of that side. In the course of his exploits, Butler became the most decorated Marine hero of his day. But by the time he retired from the military thirty-three years after he enlisted, Butler was thoroughly sickened by war and by what America demanded of its soldiers in the hellholes of empire.

He and his fellow Marines had been called upon to brutally put down wars of national liberation all over the world, from the Far East to the Caribbean. And, as Butler came to realize, there was nothing patriotic or noble about what his leathernecks had been ordered to do.

In enforcing America's will and commercial claims, Butler's men engaged in the inevitable crimes and savagery of imperial war—torching villages, subjecting insufficiently compliant peasants to baroque forms of torture, raping women, and orphaning children. Butler knew that these grimy wars took as much from his fighting men's souls as it did from their bodies. And the bloodletting was all about the filthy dollar, not about freedom or justice or the American Way, or any of the other self-aggrandizing claims of presidents and secretaries of state.

"I spent 33 years and four months in active military service and during that period I spent most of my time as a high class muscle man for Big Business, for Wall Street, and the bankers," Butler wrote, in 1935, in a bracingly honest article for a left-wing magazine called *Common Sense*. "In short, I was a racketeer, a gangster for capitalism. I helped make Mexico safe for American oil interests. I helped make Haiti and Cuba a decent place for National City Bank boys to collect revenues. I helped in the raping of a dozen Central American republics for the benefit of Wall Street. I helped purify Nicaragua for the international banking house of Brown Brothers in 1902–1912. I brought light to the Dominican Republic for the American sugar interests in 1916. I helped make Honduras right for the American fruit companies in 1903. In China in 1927, I helped see to it that Standard Oil went on its way unmolested. . . . Looking back on it, I feel I might have given Al Capone a few hints. The best he could do was to operate in three city districts. We Marines operated on three *continents*."

Butler's blunt truth-telling about what President Eisenhower would later label "the military-industrial complex" was all the more remarkable because he came from a Philadelphia family of influential politicians and bankers. Although the blue-blooded Butlers were Quakers, Smedley's father—the powerful Republican congressman Thomas Butler—saw nothing wrong with using his seat on the Naval Affairs Committee to push for a bigger US war machine. But after he finally quit the Marines—leaving the service with the rank of major general, the highest rank of the time—Smedley would become one of the country's toughest and best-known critics of the American war lobby.

Butler always stayed loyal to his former troops, risking his reputation by speaking before the Bonus Army encampment in Washington in July 1932—the ragtag assembly of World War I veterans who had occupied the nation's capital to demand reimbursement for their military service. The protestors were later violently routed by troops under the command of another military legend, General Douglas MacArthur, assisted by his young aide Dwight Eisenhower (to Ike's everlasting shame).

Butler crisscrossed the country, championing veterans' rights and stumping for peace. He was appalled to see how shabbily veterans were treated—especially those who had sustained lifelong physical and mental wounds and were warehoused in federal hospitals that Butler called graveyards of "the living dead." In Indiana, the general came upon a particularly dismal facility where hundreds of shell-shocked veterans were held in old barracks that Butler compared to "pens" for rabid dogs.

The crusading Marine was determined that the United States should never again maim a generation of America's finest in a war of greed—and then discard these young men like spent cartridges. He poured his grief and outrage into his classic 1935 jeremiad *War Is a Racket*. If the United States ever went to war again, he argued in the book, this time it should be fought by the rich and powerful. The First World War had created over twenty thousand new millionaires, he pointed out. How many of these war profiteers "shouldered a rifle," he acidly observed. "How many of them spent sleepless, frightened nights, ducking shells and shrapnel and machine-gun bullets?"

Butler never cashed in on war, never joined the boards of defense companies like other retired generals. After taking off his uniform, he supported his family by writing and speaking—giving away half of what he made to veterans' causes. He remained so popular among rank-and-file soldiers that a group of wealthy conspirators approached him in 1933 about leading another Bonus Army–type march on Washington—this time with *armed* veterans—to overthrow President Franklin Delano Roosevelt. FDR had antagonized powerful Wall Street banking interests as well as right-wing manufacturers like the Du Ponts with his New Deal reforms. Only a man like Butler, the conspirators concluded, commanded enough respect to make former soldiers follow his lead. But instead of succumbing to the dazzling lures of money and power, Butler followed his conscience. And in dramatic testimony before a congressional committee in November 1934, the general again became a hero, exposing the plot against FDR and saving American democracy.

Butler's inspirational life story and antiwar passion remain as relevant as ever today. A state of permanent war has become the norm in America. During the Cold War, American democracy had to contend with the growing power of the military-industrial sector. But during the endless War on Terror—a war that expands with every murky group and remote region that Washington declares our enemy—it's the entire nation that has become militarized. The eyes of the surveillance state are everywhere, flag-waving patriotism is more compulsory than ever, and more and more boys are encouraged to dream of war. Movie posters across the land celebrate armed men pumped up with steroids and fury; video games wallow in gore and cold-blooded snipers become cult icons; sports fans are compelled to again and again honor our troops, to cheer the rockets' red glare and God-graced America and the roar of Air Force flyovers; political office seekers vie to be the toughest on the block when it comes to punishing downtrodden, brown-skinned populations in the Middle East and reviving the Cold War against Russia.

And yet for all this aggression surging through the body politic, and for all the "honor" we heap on our troops, in reality we don't give much of a damn for the plight of our soldiers. We don't really want to know much about what is happening over there, in our name, in those forsaken desert battlegrounds. And when our fighting men and women return home, we begrudge them their benefits, even when they're sick and damaged from war.

This is the sorry state of our war-obsessed, blood-saturated nation today. It was nearly half a century ago when Martin Luther

King Jr. warned America about the violent path down which it was headed. "A nation that continues year after year to spend more money on military defense than on programs of social uplift is approaching spiritual death," declared King. Today—nearly fifty years after King himself fell victim to gunfire—the United States remains more deeply enthralled by the reign of violence and death than ever.

We desperately need visionaries and angels of our better nature like King to help lead us back to the light. And we need men and women like Smedley Darlington Butler, warriors who marched and fought bravely under the Stars and Stripes—only to realize that the more noble battle was at home, for America's soul. Boys still dream of war. But men and women must dream of peace.

David Talbot is the founder of Salon.com, and the editorial director of Hot Books/Skyhorse. He is the author of the *New York Times* best-seller *The Devil's Chessboard: Allen Dulles, the CIA and the Rise of America's Secret Government.*

Introduction

By Jesse Ventura

In my humble opinion, this little book should be required reading for every high school history classroom in America. *War Is a Racket* was written in 1935, but don't let that fool you. It's as relevant today—three-quarters of a century later—as it was then. Maybe even more so. There's an old saying, "The more things change, the more they stay the same," and Smedley Butler's hard-hitting assessment continues to hold a vital message to be heeded in our time.

The General was a man after my own heart. Having served honorably in the military—as I did as a Navy frogman—he knows whereof he speaks when it comes to war. He understands the soldiers who fight for their country. And he came to realize—and be outraged by—those making another kind of killing off of their blood, sweat, and tears.

You need to know some background about Smedley Butler in order to fully appreciate what you're about to read. He was born in 1881 to a prominent Quaker family in Pennsylvania, the oldest of three sons. His grandfather and later his father were elected to U.S. Congress. A fine athlete in high school, he left against his father's wishes shortly before his seventeenth birthday to enlist in the Marines after the Spanish-American War broke out. Lying about his age, Butler received a direct commission as a second lieutenant.

He had contempt for red tape, worked devotedly alongside his men, and rose quickly in the ranks. Butler went on to take part in just about all the U.S. military actions of his time: in Cuba and Manila, then the Boxer Rebellion in China (where he was twice wounded in action and promoted to captain at only nineteen), and then a series of interventions in Central America and the Caribbean. Those were known as the "Banana Wars," because the aim was to protect the Panama Canal and U.S. commercial interests in the region such as the United Fruit Company.

At only thirty-seven, Butler became a brigadier general. In command of a camp in France during World War I,

> "[T]he ground under the tents was nothing but mud, [so] he had raided the wharf at Brest of the duckboards no longer needed for the trenches, carted the first one himself up that four-mile hill to the camp, and thus provided something in the way of protection for the men to sleep on." [1]

That's the kind of guy Smedley Butler was.

He took some time off in the Roaring Twenties to become director of public safety in Philadelphia; running the city's po-

---

[1] Quote spoken by Novelist Mary Roberts Rinehart, after receiving a letter from U.S. Secretary of War Newton Baker.

lice and fire departments. There his no-bullshit style got him into some trouble. The municipal government and its cops were unbelievably corrupt, and from the get-go, Butler was raiding speakeasies while cracking down on prostitution and gambling. Let's say he wasn't too popular among the rich and powerful who were used to law enforcement turning a blind eye in exchange for their payoffs.

Plus, perish the thought, the general often swore while giving his regular radio talks. When the mayor told the press, "I had the guts to bring General Butler to Philadelphia and I have the guts to fire him," a crowd of four thousand Smedley supporters came together and forced a truce to keep him in Philadelphia awhile longer. Resigning after nearly two tumultuous years as director of public safety, Butler later said, "Cleaning up Philadelphia was worse than any battle I was ever in."

During the late 1920s, Butler commanded a Marine Expeditionary Force in China and was named a major general upon his return. Nicknamed "The Fighting Quaker," Butler had been hailed as "the outstanding American soldier" by Theodore Roosevelt. He is one of only nineteen people to this day who have been twice awarded the Medal of Honor. He also received the Marine Corps Brevet Medal, the highest Marine decoration at the time for officers. All told, Smedley served thirty-four years in the Marine Corps before retiring from active duty in 1931, at the age of fifty. When he became a civilian, the man had been under fire more than 120 times. He gave his men maps of how to get to his house, in case they ever needed him for anything.

That was around the same time Butler had landed in hot water with President Herbert Hoover for publicly stating some gossip about Italian dictator Benito Mussolini, who it was alleged had been involved in a hit-and-run accident on a young child. When the Italian government protested, if you can believe it, Hoover asked his secretary of the Navy to court-martial Butler! For the first time since the Civil War, a general officer was placed under arrest; confined to his post! A man with eighteen decorations—outrageous! But I guess our appeasement of Fascist dictators isn't anything new. President Franklin D. Roosevelt, then governor of New York, volunteered to testify on Butler's behalf, and ultimately, Butler got off with a "reprimand" and his court-martial withdrawn.

But Smedley wasn't about to go "gentle into that good night," as Dylan Thomas's famous poem states. He'd been a good soldier, following the orders of his superiors—like when the Taft Administration asked him to help rig elections in Nicaragua. But in the course of his service, he'd seen too much and started giving lectures about what he'd observed, donating much of the money that he earned to unemployment relief in his Philadelphia hometown, as we were then in the midst of the Great Depression.

In 1931, a speech Butler delivered before the American Legion made the papers. In it, he said:

> "I spent thirty-three years and four months in active military service, and during that period I spent most of my time being a high-class muscle man for Big Business, for Wall Street and the bankers. In short, I was a racketeer, a gangster for capitalism. I helped make Honduras

right for the American fruit companies in 1903. I helped purify Nicaragua for the International Banking House of Brown Brothers in 1902–1912. I helped make Mexico and especially Tampico safe for American oil interests in 1914. I brought light to the Dominican Republic for the American sugar interests in 1916. I helped make Haiti and Cuba a decent place for the National City Bank boys to collect revenues in. I helped in the raping of half a dozen Central American republics for the benefit of Wall Street. In China in 1927 I helped see to it that Standard Oil went on its way unmolested. Looking back on it, I might have given Al Capone a few hints. The best he could do was to operate his racket in three districts. I operated on three continents."

Wow! You don't think that raised some hackles? (And probably had some folks wanting to put Smedley in shackles.) Deciding to run for the U.S. Senate, Butler spoke out strongly on behalf of the World War I veterans who'd never been paid their promised bonuses. When their "Bonus Army" set up a protest camp in Washington, DC, in 1932, Butler showed up with his young son to cheer the men on; this was the night before the Hoover Administration was preparing to evict them. He walked through the camp telling the vets they'd served honorably and had as much right to lobby Congress as any corporation did. He and his son ate with the men and spent the night. But before the month was out, General Douglas MacArthur came charging in with an Army cavalry, destroying the camp. Several vets were injured or killed during the melee. Smedley Butler was furious; he didn't make it into the Senate, but he switched parties and voted for FDR for president.

And he wasn't done making waves . . . of tidal proportions. On November 30, 1934, Butler testified before a House committee in closed-door executive session. The story then leaked in three newspapers, and began: "Major General Smedley D. Butler revealed today that he had been asked by a group of wealthy New York brokers to lead a Fascist movement to set up a dictatorship in the United States."

You can read the whole story in a book called *The Plot to Seize the White House* by Jules Archer, which is still in print. I did a summary of it in my earlier book, *American Conspiracies*. It's a classic story of the power broker mind-set; that if you tempt someone with a big enough offer, they can't help but come over to your side. Not Smedley Butler. He had too much integrity.

Here was the thing: President Roosevelt's New Deal was considered downright anti-American and evil by the Wall Street crowd (as it still is blamed today by the radicals passing themselves off as legitimate conservatives). The president was taking on the stock speculators and setting up new watchdog federal agencies. He was putting a halt on farm foreclosures and forcing employers to accept union collective bargaining. He took the nation off the gold standard, which meant more paper money would be available to provide loans and create jobs for the millions of unemployed. Lo and behold, he even spoke of raising taxes on the rich to help pay for New Deal programs.

So a lot of titans of finance hated the man's guts. Butler even suspected some of them might have been behind a failed assassination attempt against him shortly before he was elected president. Then one day in 1934, to Butler's surprise, a bond salesman named Gerry MacGuire approached him. The retired general smelled a rat, but decided to play along until he could figure out what was really going on. He let MacGuire court him for some months. The fellow turned out to be employed by financier Grayson Murphy.

Butler was told by MacGuire that some really important people with plenty of money wanted to establish a new organization. They had $3 million in working capital and as much as *$300 million* which they could tap into. Butler realized the truth of this when some captains of industry came together and announced they were forming a new American Liberty League that September. Its stated goals were "to combat radicalism, to teach the necessity of respect for the rights of persons and property, and generally to foster free private enterprise." The League's backers included Rockefellers, Mellons, and Pews, as well as two unsuccessful Democratic presidential candidates, John W. Davis (an attorney for the Morgan banking interests) and Al Smith (a business associate of the DuPonts).

MacGuire arranged to put Butler back in touch with a fellow he'd once served alongside, Robert S. Clark, an heir to the Singer Sewing Machine fortune and a by-now wealthy banker. Butler later remembered Clark saying, "You know, the president is weak. . . . He was raised in this class, and he will come back. . . . But we have got to be prepared to sustain him when he does."

So who was their choice to lead a government takeover? That's right, Smedley Butler. They knew how popular he was with veterans, and the idea was to have Smedley come out of retirement and lead another veterans' "Bonus Army" march on the nation's capital. They wanted to create havoc with as many as five hundred thousand men at Butler's heels. Pressured by these events, so the twisted thinking went, FDR would be convinced to name Butler to a new cabinet post as a secretary of "general affairs" or "general welfare." Eventually, the president would agree to turn over the reins of power to Butler altogether, under the excuse that his polio was worsening, and FDR would become a mere ceremonial figurehead.

You need to remember that this was the same time as Hitler's rise to power in Germany and Mussolini's consolidation of his dictatorship in Italy, so such ideas were very much in the air. But they picked the wrong coup d' dude in Butler. Smedley decided to bring a reporter friend in on the conspiracy, so it wouldn't be just his word against the plotters', and they worked together to gather more background.

After his testimony before the House McCormack-Dickstein Committee around Thanksgiving of 1934, the *New York Times* ran a front-page story with a two-column headline: "Gen. Butler Bares 'Fascist Plot' To Seize Government by Force." But most of the article was full of denials and outright ridicule from some of the bigwigs that he'd implicated, while the meat of Smedley's charges got buried on an inside page. *Time* magazine followed up with a piece headlined "Plot without Plotters," complete with a cartoon of Butler riding a white horse and asking veterans to follow him. "No military officer of the United States since the late tempestuous George Custer has succeeded in publicly floundering in so much hot water as Smedley Darlington Butler," the article said. Doesn't seem like the big media have changed their spots much over the last eighty years, does it?

The House committee went ahead with mounting an investigation, which lasted for two months. They verified that Butler had been offered an $18,000 bribe—no paltry sum in those days—and a number of other facts. The Veterans of Foreign Wars commander, James Van Zandt, revealed that he, too, had been approached by "agents of Wall Street" to lead a Fascist dictatorship. Even *Time* came out with a small-print "footnote" that the committee was "convinced . . . that General Butler's story of a Fascist march on Washington was alarmingly true."

But then the committee's investigation came to a sudden stop and none of the alleged financiers were ever called for questioning. In fact, when the transcript of the committee's interview with Butler came out, every person he'd named ended up being deleted. "Not a single participant will be prosecuted under the perfectly plain language of the federal conspiracy act making this a high crime," said the ACLU's Roger Baldwin. I can't help but think of the current administration in Washington refusing to even consider prosecuting the Bush people for their involvement in torture.

When John McCormack, who chaired the committee and went on to become House Speaker, was interviewed years later about what had happened, he claimed he couldn't remember why they'd avoided going after the bankers and other corporate powers. McCormack did say in 1971:

"If the plotters had got rid of Roosevelt, there's no telling what might have taken place. They wouldn't have
told the people what they were doing, of course. They
were going to make it all sound constitutional, of course,
with a high-sounding name for the dictator and a plan
to make it all sound like a good American program. A
well-organized minority can always outmaneuver an un-
organized majority, as Adolf Hitler did. . . . The people
were in a very confused state of mind, making the nation
weak and ripe for some drastic kind of extremist reac-
tion. Mass frustration could bring about anything."

That, again, feels to me like we're in a déjà vu today.

Smedley Butler didn't live a whole lot longer. He died at age
fifty-eight on June 21, 1940, in the Naval Hospital in Philadelphia, after becoming ill with probable stomach cancer a few weeks
earlier. But he left us all an amazing legacy in this book, *War Is a
Racket*. It's an anti-war classic by a man who knew firsthand what
he was talking about.

Like Smedley, I enlisted against my father's wishes, going into
the Navy right after I finished high school. Every member of my
immediate family is a war veteran. My father had seven Bronze
Battle Stars in World War II. My mother was an Army nurse in
North Africa. My brother is a Vietnam veteran. So I know whereof
I speak, too, when I stand with General Butler against America's
ongoing imperialist wars. I opposed the invasion of Iraq from day
one, because we were lining our military up against another sov-
ereign nation as an aggressor and an occupier. And who benefited

from our lying our way into Iraq? The Halliburtons of this world, the war profiteer contractors and their banker backers.

Here's the way Butler puts it in chapter 3 of *War Is a Racket*:

> "Beautiful ideals were painted for our boys who were sent out to die. This was the 'war to end wars.' This was the 'war to make the world safe for democracy.' No one told them that dollars and cents were the real reason."

He also points out that our national debt—such a rallying cry today—is directly tied big-time to "our fiddling in international affairs."

> "We are paying it, our children will pay it, and our children's children probably still will be paying the cost of that war."

And he was talking then about World War I!

I also resonated strongly with Butler's noting the terrible dichotomy between those who promote these wars and those who must fight them. "How many of these war millionaires shouldered a rifle?" he writes. "How many of them were wounded or killed in battle?"

This goes along with something I've proposed in the past. If I ever became president, I'd push with every ounce of power I had for Congress to pass this into law:

> Every elected federal official must pre-designate an individual in their immediate family who has to begin military service—the moment that official casts an affirmative vote toward going to war. This could be a grandchild, a niece or nephew, but someone. It doesn't mean they necessarily go to the war zone. What it does mean is that they and their family experience some personal discomfort because of this decision. Going to war *should* bring difficulty, especially to those who are the orchestrators or the authorizers. Right now, it's far too easy for them to go on TV with their bleeding hearts and give standing ovations to our service personnel. War should not be laissez-faire. If you're not willing to send someone from your family, how can you be so willing to send someone else's?

All in all, *War Is a Racket* demands a contemporary audience. We need real heroes for our young people to emulate, individuals who weren't afraid to take a stand for the sake of our country. I believe the story—and the words—of General Butler need to be as widely known as those of Washington and Lincoln. If this means making us think about the fact that wealthy people can sometimes be out for evil purposes, let the chips fall where they may. Thank you, General Butler, for your inspiration!

Jesse Ventura

CHAPTER ONE

War Is a Racket!

WAR is a racket. It always has been. It is possibly the oldest, easily the most profitable, surely the most vicious. It is the only one international in scope. It is the only one in which the profits are reckoned in dollars and the losses in lives.

A racket is best described, I believe, as something that is not what it seems to the majority of people. Only a small "inside" group knows what it is about. It is conducted for the benefit of the very few, at the expense of the very many. Out of war a few people make huge fortunes.

In the World War a mere handful garnered the profits of the conflict. At least 21,000 new millionaires and billionaires were made in the United States during the World War. That many admitted their huge blood gains in their income tax returns. How many other war millionaires falsified their income tax returns no one knows.

How many of these war millionaires shouldered a rifle? How many of them dug a trench? How many of them knew what it meant to go hungry in a rat-infested dugout? How many of them spent sleepless, frightened nights, ducking shells and shrapnel and machine gun bullets? How many of them parried the bayonet thrust of an enemy? How many of them were wounded or killed in battle?

Out of war nations acquire additional territory, if they are victorious. They just take it. This newly acquired territory promptly is exploited by the few—the self-same few who wrung dollars out of blood in the war. The general public shoulders the bill.

And what is this bill?

This bill renders a horrible accounting. Newly placed gravestones. Mangled bodies. Shattered minds. Broken hearts and homes. Economic instability. Depression and all its attendant miseries. Back-breaking taxation for generations and generations.

For a great many years, as a soldier, I had a suspicion that war was a racket; not until I retired to civil life did I fully realize it. Now that I see the international war clouds again gathering, as they are today, I must face it and speak out.

Again they are choosing sides. France and Russia met and agreed to stand side by side. Italy and Austria hurried to make a similar agreement. Poland and Germany cast sheep's eyes at each other, forgetting, for the nonce, their dispute over the Polish Corridor. The assassination of King Alexander of Yugoslavia complicated matters. Yugoslavia and Hungary, long bitter enemies, were almost at each other's throats. Italy was ready to jump in. But France was waiting. So was Czechoslovakia. All of them are looking ahead to war. Not the people—not those who fight and pay and die—only those who foment wars and remain safely at home to profit.

There are 40,000,000 men under arms in the world today, and our statesmen and diplomats have the temerity to say that war is not in the making.

Hell's bells! Are these 40,000,000 men being trained to be dancers?

Not in Italy, to be sure. Premier Mussolini knows what they are being trained for. He, at least, is frank enough to speak out. Only the other day, Il Duce in "International Conciliation," the publication of the Carnegie Endowment for International Peace, said:

And, above all, Fascism, the more it considers and observes the future and the development of humanity quite apart from political considerations of the moment, believes neither in the possibility for the utility of perpetual peace. . . War alone brings up to its highest tension all human energy and puts the stamp of nobility upon the peoples who have the courage to meet it.

Undoubtedly Mussolini means exactly what he says. His well trained army, his great fleet of planes, and even his navy are ready for war—anxious for it, apparently. His recent stand at the side of Hungary in the latter's dispute with Yugoslavia showed that. And the hurried mobilization of his troops on the Austrian border after the assassination of Dollfuss showed it too. There are others in Europe too whose sabre-rattling presages war, sooner or later.

Herr Hitler, with his rearming Germany and his constant demands for more and more arms, is an equal if not a greater menace to peace. France only recently increased the term of military service for its youth from a year to eighteen months.

Yes, all over, nations are camping on their arms. The mad dogs of Europe are on the loose.

In the Orient the maneuvering is more adroit. Back in 1904, when Russian and Japan fought, we kicked out our old friends the Russians and backed Japan. Then our very generous international bankers were financing Japan. Now the trend is to poison us against the Japanese. What does the "open door" policy in China mean to us? Our trade with China is about $90,000,000 a year. Or the Philippine Islands? We have spent about $600,000,000 in the Philippines in 35 years and we (our bankers and industrials and speculators) have private investments there of less than $200,000,000.

Then, to save that China trade of about $90,000,000, or to protect these private investments of less than $200,000,000 in the Philippines, we would be all stirred up to hate Japan and go to war—a war that might well cost us tens of billions of dollars, hundreds of thousands of lives of Americans, and many more hundreds of thousands of physically maimed and mentally unbalanced men.

Of course, for this loss, there would be a compensating profit—fortunes would be made. Millions and billions of dollars would be piled up. By a few. Munitions makers. Ship builders. Manufacturers. Meat packers. Speculators. They would fare well.

Yes, they are getting ready for another war. Why shouldn't they? It pays high dividends.

But what does it profit the masses?

What does it profit the men who are killed? What does it profit the men who are maimed? What does it profit their mothers and sisters, their wives and their sweethearts? What does it profit their children?

What does it profit anyone except the very few to whom war means huge profits?

Yes, and what does it profit the nation?

Take our own case. Until 1898 we didn't own a bit of territory outside the mainland of North America. At that time our national debt was a little more than $1,000,000,000. Then we became "internationally minded." We forgot, or shunted aside, the advice of the Father of our Country. We forgot Washington's warning about "entangling alliances." We went to war. We acquired outside territory. At the end of the World War period, as a direct result of our fiddling in international affairs, our national debt had jumped to over $25,000,000,000. Therefore, on a purely financial bookkeeping basis, we ran a little behind year for year, and that foreign trade might well have been ours without the wars.

It would have been far cheaper (not to say safer) for the average American who pays the bills to stay out of foreign entanglements. For a very few this racket, like bootlegging and other underworld rackets, brings fancy profits, but the cost of operations is always transferred to the people—who do not profit.

CHAPTER TWO

Who Makes the Profits?

The World War, rather our brief participation in it, has cost the United States some $52,000,000,000. Figure it out. That means $400 to every American man, woman, and child. And we haven't paid the debt yet. We are paying it, our children will pay it, and our children's children probably still will be paying the cost of that war.

The normal profits of a business concern in the United States are six, eight, ten, and sometimes even twelve per cent. But war-time profits—ah! that is another matter—twenty, sixty, one hundred, three hundred, and even eighteen hundred per cent—the sky is the limit. All that the traffic will bear. Uncle Sam has the money. Let's get it.

Of course, it isn't put that crudely in war time. It is dressed into speeches about patriotism, love of country, and "we must all put our shoulder to the wheel," but the profits jump and leap and skyrocket—and are safely pocketed. Let's just take a few examples:

Take our friend the du Ponts, the powder people—didn't one of them testify before a Senate committee recently that their powder won the war? Or something? How did they do in the war? They were a patriotic corporation. Well, the average earnings of the du Ponts for the period 1910 to 1914 was $6,000,000 a year.

It wasn't much, but the du Ponts managed to get along on it. Now let's look at their average yearly profit during the war years, 1914 to 1918.

Fifty-eight million dollars a year profit, we find! Nearly ten times that of normal times, and the profits of normal times were pretty good. An increase in profits of more than 950 per cent.

Take one of our little steel companies that so patriotically shunted aside the making of rails and girders and bridges to manufacture war materials. Well, their 1910–1914 yearly earnings averaged $6,000,000. Then came the war. And, like loyal citizens, Bethlehem Steel promptly turned to munitions making. Did their profits jump—or did they let Uncle Sam in for a bargain? Well, their 1914–1918 average was $49,000,000 a year!

Or, let's take United States Steel. The normal earnings during the five-year period prior to the war were $105,000,000 a year. Not bad. Then along came the war and up went the profits. The average yearly profit for the period 1914–1918 was $240,000,000. Not bad.

There you have some of the steel and powder earnings. Let's look at something else. A little copper, perhaps. That always does well in war times.

Anaconda, for instance. Average yearly earnings during the pre-war years 1910–1914 of $10,000,000. During the war years 1914–1918 profits leaped to $34,000,000 per year.

Or Utah Copper. Average of $5,000,000 per year during the 1910–1914 period. Jumped to average of $21,000,000 yearly profits for the war period.

Let's group these five, with three smaller companies. The total yearly average profits of the pre-war period 1910–1914 were $137,480,000. Then along came the war. The yearly average profits for this group skyrocketed to $408,300,000.

A little increase in profits of approximately 200 per cent.

Does war pay? It paid them. But they aren't the only ones. There are still others. Let's take leather.

For the three-year period before the war the total profits of Central Leather Company were $3,500,000. That was approximately $1,167,000 a year. Well, in 1916 Central Leather returned a profit of $15,500,000, a small increase of 1,100 per cent. That's all. The General Chemical Company averaged a profit for the three years before the war of a little over $800,000 a year.

Then came the war, and the profits jumped to $12,000,000. A leap of 1,400 per cent.

International Nickel Company—and you can't have a war without nickel—showed an increase in profits from a mere average of $4,000,000 a year to $73,500,000 yearly. Not bad? An increase of more than 1,700 per cent.

American Sugar Refining Company averaged $200,000 a year for the three years before the war. In 1916 a profit of $6,000,000 was recorded.

Listen to Senate Document No. 259. The Sixty-Fifth Congress, reporting on corporate earnings and government revenues. Considering the profits of 122 meat packers, 153 cotton manufactures, 299 garment makers, 49 steel plants, and 340 coal producers during the war. Profits under 25 per cent were exceptional. For instance, the coal companies made between 100 per cent and

7,856 per cent on their capital stock during the war. The Chicago packers doubled and tripled their earnings.

And let us not forget the bankers who financed this great war. If anyone had the cream of the profits it was the bankers. Being partnerships rather than incorporated organization, they do not have to report to stockholders. And their profits were as secret as they were immense. How the bankers made their millions and their billions I do not know, because those little secrets never become public—even before a Senate investigatory body.

But here's how some of the other patriotic industrialists and speculators chiseled their way into war profits.

Take the shoe people. They like war. It brings business with abnormal profits. They made huge profits on sales abroad to our allies. Perhaps, like the munitions manufacturers and armament makers, they also sold to the enemy. For a dollar is a dollar whether it comes from Germany or from France. But they did well by Uncle Sam too. For instance, they sold Uncle Sam 35,000,000 pairs of hobnailed service shoes. There were 4,000,000 soldiers. Eight pairs, and more, to a soldier. My regiment during the war had only a pair to a soldier. Some of these shoes probably are still in existence. They were good shoes. But when the war was over Uncle Sam had a matter of 25,000,000 pairs left over. Bought—and paid for. Profits recorded and pocketed.

There was still lots of leather left. So the leather people sold your Uncle Sam hundreds of thousands of McClellan saddles for the cavalry. But there wasn't any American cavalry overseas! Somebody had to get rid of this leather, however. Somebody had to make a profit on it—so we had a lot of those McClellan saddles. And we probably have those yet.

Also somebody had a lot of mosquito netting. They sold your Uncle Sam 20,000,000 mosquito nets for the use of the soldiers overseas. I suppose the boys were expected to put it over them as they tried to sleep in the muddy trenches—one hand scratching cooties on their backs and the other making passes at scurrying rats. Well, not one of these mosquito nets ever got to France!

Anyhow, these thoughtful manufacturers wanted to make sure that no soldier would be without his mosquito net, so 40,000,000 additional yards of mosquito netting were sold to Uncle Sam.

There were pretty good profits in mosquito netting in war days, even if there were no mosquitoes in France.

I suppose, if the war had lasted just a little longer, the enterprising mosquito netting manufacturers would have sold your Uncle Sam a couple of consignments of mosquitoes to plant in France so that more mosquito netting would be in order.

Airplane and engine manufacturers felt they, too, should get their just profits out of this war. Why not? Everybody else was getting theirs. So $1,000,000,000—count them if you live long enough—was spent by Uncle Sam in building airplanes and airplane engines that never left the ground! Not one plane, or motor, out of the billion dollars' worth ordered, ever got into a battle in France. Just the same the manufacturers made their little profit of 30, 100 or perhaps 300 per cent.

Undershirts for soldiers cost 14 cents to make and Uncle Sam paid 30 cents to 40 cents each for them—a nice little profit for the undershirt manufacturer. And the stocking manufacturers and the uniform manufacturers and the cap manufacturers and the steel helmet manufacturers—all got theirs.

Why, when the war was over some 4,000,000 sets of equipment—knapsacks and the things that go to fill them—crammed warehouses on this side. Now they are being scrapped because the regulations have changed the contents. But the manufacturers collected their wartime profits on them—and they will do it all over again the next time.

There were lots of brilliant ideas for profit making during the war.

One very versatile patriot sold Uncle Sam twelve dozen 48-inch wrenches. Oh, they were very nice wrenches. The only trouble was that there was only one nut ever made that was large enough for these wrenches. That is the one that holds the turbines at Niagara Falls! Well, after Uncle Sam had bought them and the manufacturer had pocketed the profit, the wrenches were put on freight cars and shunted all around the United States in an effort to find a use for them. When the Armistice was signed it was indeed a sad blow to the wrench manufacturer. He was just about to make some nuts to fit the wrenches. Then he planned to sell these, too, to your Uncle Sam.

Still another had the brilliant idea that colonels shouldn't ride in automobiles, nor should they even ride horseback. One had probably seen a picture of Andy Jackson riding on a buckboard. Well, some 6,000 buckboards were sold to Uncle Sam for the use of colonels! Not one of them was used. But the buckboard manufacturer got his war profit.

The shipbuilders felt they should come in on some of it, too. They built a lot of ships that made a lot of profit. More than $3,000,000,000 worth. Some to the ships were all right. But $635,000,000 worth of them were made of wood and wouldn't float! The seams opened up—and they sank. We paid for them, though. And somebody pocketed the profits.

It has been estimated by statisticians and economists and researchers that the war cost your Uncle Sam $52,000,000,000. Of this sum, $39,000,000,000 was expended in the actual war period. This expenditure yielded $16,000,000,000 in profits. That is how the 21,000 billionaires and millionaires got that way. This $16,000,000,000 profits is not to be sneezed at. It is quite a tidy sum. And it went to a very few.

The Senate (Nye) committee probe of the munitions industry and its wartime profits, despite its sensational disclosures, hardly has scratched the surface.

Even so, it has had some effect. The State Department has been studying "for some time" methods of keeping out of war. The War Department suddenly decides it has a wonderful plan to spring. The Administration names a committee—with the War and Navy Departments ably represented under the chairmanship of a Wall Street speculator—to limit profits in war time. To what extent isn't suggested. Hmmm. Possibly the profits of 300 and 600 and 1,600 per cent of those who turned blood into gold in the World War would be limited to some smaller figure.

Apparently, however, the plan does not call for any limitation of losses—that is, the losses of those who fight the war. As far as I have been able to ascertain there is nothing in the scheme to limit a soldier to the loss of but one eye, or one arm, or to limit his wounds to one or two or three. Or to limit the loss of life.

There is nothing in this scheme, apparently, that says not more than twelve per cent of a regiment shall be wounded in battle, or that not more than seven per cent in a division should be killed.

Of course, the committee cannot be bothered with such trifling matters.

CHAPTER THREE

Who Pays the Bills?

WHO provides the profits—these nice little profits of 20, 100, 300, 1,500, and 1,800 per cent? We all pay them—in taxation. We paid the bankers their profits when we bought Liberty Bonds at $100 and sold them back at $84 or $86 to the banker. These bankers collected $100 plus. It was a simple manipulation. The bankers control the security marts. It was easy for them to depress the price of these bonds. Then all of us—the people—got frightened and sold the bonds at $84 or $86. The bankers bought them. Then these same bankers stimulated a boom and government bonds went to par—and above. Then the bankers collected their profits.

But the soldier pays the biggest part of the bill.

If you don't believe this, visit the American cemeteries on the battlefields abroad. Or visit any of the veterans' hospitals in the United States. On a tour of the country, in the midst of which I am at the time of this writing, I have visited eighteen government hospitals for veterans. In them are a total of about 50,000 destroyed men—men who were the pick of the nation eighteen years ago. The very able chief surgeon at the government hospital at Milwaukee, where there are 3,800 of the living dead, told me that mortality among veterans is three times as great as among those who stayed at home.

Boys with a normal viewpoint were taken out of the fields and offices and factories and classrooms and put into the ranks. There they were remolded; they were made over; they were made to "about face"; to regard murder as the order of the day. They were put shoulder to shoulder and, through mass psychology, they were entirely changed. We used them for a couple of years and trained them to think nothing at all of killing or of being killed.

Then, suddenly, we discharged them and told them to make another "about face"! This time they had to do their own readjusting, sans mass psychology, sans officers' aid and advice, sans nation-wide propaganda. We didn't need them any more. So we scattered them about without any "three-minute" or "Liberty Loan" speeches or parades.

Many, too many, of these fine young boys are eventually destroyed, mentally, because they could not make that final "about face" alone.

In the government hospital at Marion, Indiana, 1,800 of these boys are in pens! Five hundred of them in a barracks with steel bars and wires all around outside the buildings and on the porches. These already have been mentally destroyed. These boys don't even look like human beings. Oh, the looks on their faces! Physically, they are in good shape; mentally, they are gone.

There are thousands and thousands of these cases, and more and more are coming in all the time. The tremendous excitement of the war, the sudden cutting off of that excitement—the young boys couldn't stand it.

That's a part of the bill. So much for the dead—they have paid their part of the war profits. So much for the mentally and physically wounded—they are paying now their share of the war profits. But the others paid, too—they paid with heartbreaks when they tore themselves away from their firesides and their families to don the uniform of Uncle Sam—on which a profit had been made. They paid another part in the training camps where they were regimented and drilled while others took their jobs and their places in the lives of their communities. They paid for it in the trenches where they shot and were shot; where they went hungry for days at a time; where they slept in the mud and in the cold and in the rain—with the moans and shrieks of the dying for a horrible lullaby.

But don't forget—the soldier paid part of the dollars and cents bill too.

Up to and including the Spanish-American War, we had a prize system, and soldiers and sailors fought for money. During the Civil War they were paid bonuses, in many instances, before they went into service. The government, or states, paid as high as $1,200 for an enlistment. In the Spanish-American War they gave prize money. When we captured any vessels, the soldiers all got their share—at least, they were supposed to. Then it was found that we could reduce the cost of wars by taking all the prize money and keeping it, but conscripting the soldier anyway. Then the soldiers couldn't bargain for their labor. Everyone else could bargain, but the soldier couldn't.

Napoleon once said,

"All men are enamored of decorations. . . they positively hunger for them."

So, by developing the Napoleonic system—the medal business—the government learned it could get soldiers for less money, because the boys like to be decorated. Until the Civil War there were no medals. Then the Congressional Medal of Honor was handed out. It made enlistments easier. After the Civil War no new medals were issued until the Spanish-American War.

In the World War, we used propaganda to make the boys accept conscription. They were made to feel ashamed if they didn't join the army.

So vicious was this war propaganda that even God was brought into it. With few exceptions our clergymen joined in the clamor to kill, kill, kill. To kill the Germans. God is on our side.. .it is His will that the Germans be killed.

And in Germany, the good pastors called upon the Germans to kill the allies . . . to please the same God. That was a part of the general propaganda, built up to make people war conscious and murder conscious.

Beautiful ideals were painted for our boys who were sent out to die. This was the "war to end wars." This was the "war to make the world safe for democracy." No one told them that dollars and cents were the real reason. No one mentioned to them, as they marched away, that their going and their dying would mean huge war profits. No one told these American soldiers that they might be shot down by bullets made by their own brothers here. No one told them that the ships on which they were going to cross might be torpedoed by submarines built with United States patents. They were just told it was to be a "glorious adventure."

Thus, having stuffed patriotism down their throats, it was decided to make them help pay for the war, too. So, we gave them the large salary of $30 a month!

All they had to do for this munificent sum was to leave their dear ones behind, give up their jobs, lie in swampy trenches, eat canned willy (when they could get it) and kill and kill and kill . . . and be killed.

But wait!

Half of that wage (just a little more in a month than a riveter in a shipyard or a laborer in a munitions factory safe at home made in a day) was promptly taken from him to support his dependents, so that they would not become a charge upon his community. Then we made him pay what amounted to accident insurance—something the employer pays for in an enlightened state—and that cost him $6 a month. He had less than $9 a month left.

Then, the most crowning insolence of all—he was virtually blackjacked into paying for his own ammunition, clothing, and food by being made to buy Liberty Bonds at $100 and then we bought them back—when they came back from the war and couldn't find work—at $84 and $86. And the soldiers bought about $2,000,000,000 worth of those bonds!

Yes, the soldier pays the greater part of the bill. His family pays it too. They pay it in the same heart-break that he does. As he suffers, they suffer. At nights, as he lay in the trenches and watched shrapnel burst about him, they lay home in their beds and tossed sleeplessly—his father, his mother, his wife, his sisters, his brothers, his sons, and his daughters.

When he returned home minus an eye, or minus a leg or with his mind broken, they suffered too—as much as and even sometimes more than he. Yes, and they, too, contributed their dollars to the profits that the munitions makers and bankers and shipbuilders and the manufacturers and the speculators made. They, too, bought Liberty Bonds and contributed to the profit of the bankers after the Armistice in the hocus-pocus of manipulated Liberty Bond prices.

And even now the families of the wounded men and of the mentally broken and those who never were able to readjust themselves are still suffering and still paying.

CHAPTER FOUR

How to Smash this Racket!

WELL, it's a racket, all right.

A few profit—and the many pay. But there is a way to stop it. You can't end it by disarmament conferences. You can't eliminate it by peace parlays at Geneva. Well-meaning but impractical groups can't wipe it out by resolutions. It can be smashed effectively only by taking the profit out of war.

The only way to smash this racket is to conscript capital and industry and labor before the nation's manhood can be conscripted. One month before the Government can conscript the young men of the nation—it must conscript capital and industry and labor. Let the officers and the directors and the high-powered executives of our armament factories and our steel companies and our munitions makers and our shipbuilders and our airplane builders and the manufacturers of all the other things that provide profit in war time as well as the bankers and the speculators, be conscripted—to get $30 a month, the same wage as the lads in the trenches get.

Let the workers in these plants get the same wages—all the workers, all presidents, all executives, all directors, all managers, all bankers—yes, and all generals and all admirals and all officers and all politicians and all government office holders—everyone in the nation to be restricted to a total monthly income not to exceed that paid to the soldier in the trenches!

Let all these kings and tycoons and masters of business and all those workers in industry and all our senators and governors and

mayors pay half of their monthly $30 wage to their families and pay war risk insurance and buy Liberty Bonds.

Why shouldn't they?

They aren't running any risk of being killed or of having their bodies mangled or their minds shattered. They aren't sleeping in muddy trenches. They aren't hungry. The soldiers are!

Give capital and industry and labor thirty days to think it over and you will find, by that time, there will be no war. That will smash the war racket—that and nothing else.

Maybe I am a little too optimistic. Capital still has some say. So capital won't permit the taking of the profit out of war until the people—those who do the suffering and still pay the price—make up their minds that those they elect to office shall do their bidding, and not that of the profiteers.

Another step necessary in this flight to smash the war racket is a limited plebiscite to determine whether war should be declared. A plebiscite not of all the voters but merely of those who would be called upon to do the fighting and the dying. There wouldn't be very much sense in having the 76-year-old president of a munitions factory or the flat-footed head of an international banking firm or the cross-eyed manager of a uniform manufacturing plant—all of whom see visions of tremendous profits in the event of war—voting on whether the nation should go to war or not. They never would be called upon to shoulder arms—to sleep in a trench and to be shot. Only those who would be called upon to risk their lives for their country should have the privilege of voting to determine whether the nation should go to war.

There is ample precedent for restricting the voting to those affected. Many of our states have restrictions on those permitted to vote. In most, it is necessary to be able to read and write before you may vote. In some, you must own property. It would be a simple matter each year for the men coming of military age to register in their communities as they did in the draft during the World War and to be examined physically. Those who could pass and who would therefore be called upon to bear arms in the event of war would be eligible to vote in a limited plebiscite. They should be the ones to have the power to decide—and not a Congress few of whose members are within the age limit and fewer still of whom are in physical condition to bear arms. Only those who must suffer should have the right to vote.

A third step in this business of smashing the war racket is to make certain that our military forces are truly forces for defense only.

At each session of Congress the question of further naval appropriations comes up. The swivel-chair admirals of Washington (and there are always a lot of them) are very adroit lobbyists. And they are smart. They don't shout that "We need a lot of battleships to war on this nation or that nation." Oh, no. First of all, they let it be known that America is menaced by a great naval power. Almost any day, these admirals will tell you, the great fleet of this supposed enemy will strike suddenly and annihilate our 125,000,000 people. Just like that. Then they begin to cry for a larger navy. For what? To fight the enemy? Oh my, no. Oh, no. For defense purposes only.

Then, incidentally, they announce maneuvers in the Pacific. For defense. Uh, huh.

The Pacific is a great big ocean. We have a tremendous coastline on the Pacific. Will the maneuvers be off the coast, two or three hundred miles? Oh, no. The maneuvers will be two thousand, yes, perhaps even thirty-five hundred miles, off the coast.

The Japanese, a proud people, of course will be pleased beyond expression to see the United States fleet so close to Nippon's shores. Even as pleased as would be the residents of California were they to dimly discern, through the morning mist, the Japanese fleet playing at war games off Los Angeles.

The ships of our navy, it can be seen, should be specifically limited, by law, to within 200 miles of our coastline. Had that been the law in 1898 the Maine would never have gone to Havana Harbor. She never would have been blown up. There would have been no war with Spain with its attendant loss of life. Two hundred miles is ample, in the opinion of experts, for defense purposes. Our nation cannot start an offensive war if its ships can't go farther than 200 miles from the coastline. Planes might be permitted to go as far as 500 miles from the coast for purposes of reconnaissance. And the army should never leave the territorial limits of our nation.

To summarize: Three steps must be taken to smash the war racket.

We must take the profit out of war.

We must permit the youth of the land who would bear arms to decide whether or not there should be war.

We must limit our military forces to home defense purposes.

CHAPTER FIVE

To Hell With War!

I AM not such a fool as to believe that war is a thing of the past. I know the people do not want war, but there is no use in saying we cannot be pushed into another war.

Looking back, Woodrow Wilson was re-elected president in 1916 on a platform that he had "kept us out of war" and on the implied promise that he would "keep us out of war." Yet, five months later he asked Congress to declare war on Germany.

In that five-month interval the people had not been asked whether they had changed their minds. The 4,000,000 young men who put on uniforms and marched or sailed away were not asked whether they wanted to go forth to suffer and to die.

Then what caused our government to change its mind so suddenly?

Money.

An allied commission, it may be recalled, came over shortly before the war declaration and called on the President. The President summoned a group of advisers. The head of the commission spoke. Stripped of its diplomatic language, this is what he told the President and his group:

*There is no use kidding ourselves any longer. The cause of the
allies is lost. We now owe you (American bankers, American munitions makers, American manufacturers, American
speculators, American exporters) jive or six billion dollars.*

*If we lose (and without the help of the United States we
must lose) we, England, France and Italy, cannot pay back
this money. . .and Germany won't.*

So. . .

Had secrecy been outlawed as far as war negotiations were concerned, and had the press been invited to be present at that conference, or had the radio been available to broadcast the proceed-
ings, America never would have entered the World War. But this
conference, like all war discussions, was shrouded in the utmost
secrecy.

When our boys were sent off to war they were told it was a
"war to make the world safe for democracy" and a "war to end all
wars."

Well, eighteen years after, the world has less of a democracy
than it had then. Besides, what business is it of ours whether Russia or Germany or England or France or Italy or Austria live under
democracies or monarchies? Whether they are Fascists or Communists? Our problem is to preserve our own democracy.

And very little, if anything, has been accomplished to assure
us that the World War was really the war to end all wars.

Yes, we have had disarmament conferences and limitations of
arms conferences. They don't mean a thing. One has just failed;
the results of another have been nullified. We send our profession-

al soldiers and our sailors and our politicians and our diplomats to these conferences. And what happens?

The professional soldiers and sailors don't want to disarm. No admiral wants to be without a ship. No general wants to be without a command. Both mean men without jobs. They are not for disarmament. They cannot be for limitations of arms. And at all these conferences, lurking in the background but all-powerful, just the same, are the sinister agents of those who profit by war. They see to it that these conferences do not disarm or seriously limit armaments.

The chief aim of any power at any of these conferences has been not to achieve disarmament in order to prevent war but rather to endeavor to get more armament for itself and les s for any potential foe.

There is only one way to disarm with any semblance of practicability. That is for all nations to get together and scrap every ship, every gun, every rifle, every tank, every war plane. Even this, if it were at all possible, would not be enough.

The next war, according to experts, will be fought not with battleships, not by artillery, not with rifles and not with guns. It will be fought with deadly chemicals and gases.

Secretly each nation is studying and perfecting newer and ghastlier means of annihilating its foes wholesale. Yes, ships will continue to get built, for the shipbuilders must make their profits. And guns still will be manufactured and powder and rifles will be made, for the munitions makers must make their huge profits. And the soldiers, of course, must wear uniforms, for the manufacturers must make their war profits too.

But victory or defeat will be determined by the skill and ingenuity of our scientists.

If we put them to work making poison gas and more and more fiendish mechanical and explosive instruments of destruction, they will have no time for the constructive job of building a greater prosperity for all peoples. By putting them to this useful job, we can all make more money out of peace than we can out of war—even the munition makers.

So . . . I say, "TO HELL WITH WAR!"

SPEECHES

Memorial Day Speech (1931)

MEMORIAL DAY with its sad and sacred memories is here again. As each new Memorial Day comes around, we recall anew the great and tragic events that made the occasion for that day.

MEMORIAL DAY is one of the most SIGNIFICANT and BEAUTIFUL occasions of the year. It shows the sentiment of the people towards those who gave their lives for a GOOD cause, and it teaches a lesson in patriotism which is without parallel. MEMORIAL DAY cannot be TOO TENDERLY revered by old and young, by those who participated in any of the nation's great struggles, or by those who simply know of it as History. Our country each year is paying a GREATER tribute of respect to the soldiers—living and dead—and it is a SINCERE HOPE that this rule will be explained still more in the years to come.

There is a beautiful significance in the fact that, two years after the close of the Civil War, the thoughtful women of Columbus, Mississippi, laid their offerings ALIKE on the Northern and southern Graves. When all is said, this great nation has BUT ONE Heart. This act of these thoughtful women inspired the famous lyric of Francis Miles Finch, "The Blue and the Grey."

The ceremony of decorating the graves of the loved ones is almost as old as mankind itself. The Greeks and Romans had ceremonies in remembrance of their dead, as well the Druids. In France they have this beautiful custom participated in by whole families. It was not until may 1868, however, that general John A. Logan, National Commander of the Grand Army of the Republic and one of the great leaders of the Civil War, issued an order to the Grand Army naming the 30th of May 1868, for the "purpose of strewing with flowers or otherwise decorating graves of comrades who died in defense of their country during the Civil War." It was the purpose of General Logan to inaugurate this observance with the hope that it would be kept up from year to year while a survivor of that great conflict remains to honor the memory of the departed. The States took up the matter immediately and in many states MEMORIAL DAY is a state Holiday, and now in accordance with the Naval Regulations it is a legal Holiday, and each year the president designates Memorial Day by a Presidential Proclamation.

The youth of America should be thought through its schools the history and sprit of American institutions. Let these schools teach them this history and inspire them with this spirit. Teach the youth that it is the highest honour to say I AM AN AMERICAN CITIZEN. Let them hear the shot that was fired at Lexington, the shot that was heard around the world. Let them catch the pearls of the Liberty Bell and the spirit of Independence Day. Let them know of Lincoln's Gettysburg address, of the victories for the preservation of the union; Let them hear again of the shining and glorious victories of Dewey at Manila, of Sampson and Schley at Santiago, of Shafter, Wood and Roosevelt in 1898, and of Pershing's massive force in France, and of glorious victories so that Democracies might live.

A famous speaker said a few years back. "I have only one sentiment for soldiers, cheers for the living and tears for the dead."

We recall with pride and gratitude how our citizens responded to the call in 1917, with a swiftness that was unheard of they sprang to arms. The flower of American youth was there. They came from schools, colleges, from offices, factories, and the farm, they became "History's Graduates" in their defense of human rights and our free institutions. Five million of them now study veterans of the World War and truly typifying American spirit, the sprit of 1776, of 1812, of 1847, of 1861, of 1898.

The same Legionnaires have taken over the duty of "Carrying on" the Memorial Day observance. Over the graves of our soldier dead they will wreathe flowers, symbols of devotion and gratitude, at these graves which are Nation's Shrine, the Mecca to which the Legionnaires journey to renew their devotion to their comrades.

We must as well honor these heroic and patriotic dead by being true men, and, as true men, by faithfully fighting the battles of our day as they fought the battles of their day.

Memorial Day Speech (1933)

Memorial Day is peculiarly dedicated to soldiers. Its exercises recall precious memories of past acts of heroism on the part of the defenders of this Nation.

Besides respectfully bowing our heads in grateful admiration of the sacrifices so willingly made by them let us not, at the same time, fail to derive lessons from the past. Let us not fail to attempt to avoid the errors which led to the need for these heroic sacrifices. Let us recognize the fundamental causes leading to war and to our sufferings in peace as well. Let us acknowledge frankly that we are now, and have been for some years, facing a national condition as devastating as any war and toward a solution of which we are still struggling. Let us admit that in our rapid growth we have forgotten our real objective and have followed false gods.

One hundred and fifty-seven years ago 56 men assembled in Philadelphia declared to the world the determination of 3,000,000 Americans to escape an intolerable economic condition by instituting a form of government designed to secure to ALL its people at all times their inalienable rights of life, liberty and the pursuit of happiness.

This is still our national determination, or at least we are so informed by speakers on patriotic occasions and during political campaigns. At any rate, on this day so particularly set apart in memory of those who gave their all to further this determination let us take stock to see just how closely we have been adhering to this ideal. In other words determine what proportion of our people are really secure in their rights and what we as citizens have done or are planning to do to further this security.

The principles of our form of government are ideal and so appealing that they have heretofore held a leading place in the hearts and minds of the distressed masses of the earth groping for relief from misery and oppression.

But we must perpetually bear in mind that the principles upon
which our form of government was built can survive only through the constant,
active interest and determined participation of the great mass of "unfavored"
people for whose benefit it ~~xxxx~~ is popularly supposed to have been designed.
Whether or not this supposition is correct our form can be made to serve
properly all our citizens equally, but only by honest, fearless and utterly
unselfish leadership, backed by massed and threatening public opinion.

A workable form being accepted success or failure in government
is entirely a question of administration and is properly measured only in
terms ~~inxixxvyx~~ of the physical and mental well-being of all its people at
all times. No form of government can survive for long if entrusted to the
forces of selfishness and dishonesty. An unbridled desire for money and power
will destroy any leadership and the continuance of dishonest leadership
will eventually wreck any form of government.

The thousands of magnificently courageous and trusting Americans
who have willingly given their lives to their country did so cheerfully
in the simple belief that their sacrifices were helping to build a huge
defensive and offensive national machine for the benefit of all both in prosperity
and in adversity.

From the beginning we have advanced steadily in importance and
keep in mind   determination
in material wealth, but let us ~~rememvy~~ our announced ~~intentipn~~ was not ~~only~~
                                                            be
~~rixinxixikixhikk~~ ~~ffxravivf~~ greatness to/measured by huge, concentrated
fortunes for a few but by the security to all of life liberty and the
pursuit of happiness.

Along with the accumulation of this material wealth we
coined impressive mottoes: "One from many"; "All to the aid of one";
"The strong to the weak"; "The rich to the poor" ; "In unity there is
strength"; "Making the World Safe for Democracy"; "War to end war."
All these catch-phrases for the consumption of the soldier while he
spilled his precious blood gathering up territory ~~ioxxdf~~ for the benefit
of concentrated wealth.

For who but soldiers gained the territory we have; we would not even be living in the United States of America today had it not been for soldiers. And I say to you that the Nation which fails to remember,honor and properly care for its soldiers will perish from the earth . ThibxBxbibmb xxx   The people of this Nation as a whole have not ceased to love and honor the memory of the soldiers and to be grateful for their sacrifices. Only those seem to have forgotten whose short-sighted vision has led them momentarily to worship the balanced budget above the morale engendered by justice to the truest and most loyal employees this Nation has ever known.

What could be better insurance against a future national disaster than conviction on the part of the masses of average citizens,xyxixv from which soldiers spring,that this is a grateful and appreciative government?

We have fought and won many wars. Our histroy is filled with acts of sublime heroism. We have endured indescribable hardships and suffering ---but have we really secured to all our people their inalienable rights of life liberty and the pursuit of happiness?

We have now nearly half the wealth of the world with but a twentieth of its population--and a fourth of our people are in dire distress if not actual hunger.

It hxxvhvxx should be apparent to all that of late years we have not really been advancing, at least not on the right road. And a nation which fails to advance, goes backward. For a people there is no such thing as standing still. We have grown big and fat perhaps, but no nation xhx is really great with a fourth of its people in urgent need.

Our Nation can be saved, and it will be; but only by the complete unhorsing of the greedy, dishonest and selfish influences which have exploited us for personal gain.

So-called leaders,self-termed patriots, have shouted from the house-tops that their conduct of affairs has been for the best interests of the country at large and while our stomachs were full we were content to let their statements go unquestioned.

Now we realize that national welfare in the eyes of such leaders is but the welfare of their own particular class and we will never emerge from this gloom until we have completely and forever rid ourselves of such people. By this means the morale of the average citizen who does the dying in war and the suffering in peace can best and most quickly be raised and his confidence restored. And we will get nowhere until this is done.

The 'unfavored' man firmly believes this can be done by his own great government, in which he still has confidence, by swift and sure action --not shadow-boxing, action that he can understand and see with his own eyes, such as the expulsion from public life of all in whom the average *man* cannot have trust.

Americans are not fools and xxxxx know when governmental action is real. They will know it is real when they hear cries of 'Kamerad' from the self-styled defenders of 'the best interests of the public,' the crowd that has always reaped the only profits/gained from war.

There has always been a Tory class in our country, a class of people xxxxv that believes the Nation, its resources and its man-power was provided by the Almighty only for its own xxxspecial use and profit. This Tory class through the shameless use of its wealth has obtained a strangle-hold xxxv on all our institutions with the present distress an indication of the result.

It will take the greatest courage on the part of true leaders to break this devastating grip, but it must be broken if our great democracy is to survive. Let us not be distracted from this paramount issue by European and other foreign problems.

The gains made by our messing in the affairs of strangers have been offset many, many times by our losses in the wars that inevitably followed such meddling. Will anyone please point out what the great masses of this country--the 'unfavored' classes from which the soldiers are drawn-- have gained by our participation in foreign wars?

. What, for instance, ‏xxxxhahxbhhxhxgahhhdbb‏ the unfortunates
compelled to work in sweatshops, the mothers of our future soldiers,
gained from any war, past present or future?

Individually men have wielded power in our country in proportion
to their wealth, have occupied space in our national picture in ‏xxcvxdauxvv‏
                                                    the
the same proportion. We have come to disregard ‏th‏ poor worker but we
must not forget that driven too far these 'unfavored' will unite with
others like themselves; and thus, united, will loom much larger than
all the 'favored' and their dollars.

Sooner or later in the history of every government an administration
must decide which side it ‏xklixtxhxx‏ is on. I have every confidence
that the President realizes all of this and that he will gradually but
surely swing the axe on the rotten dead-wood of our discredited financial
set-up, and lead us along the road where the life ,liberty and pursuit
of happiness of all Americans is considered long before the importance
                        lead us
of the dollar—to the land where the welfare of the man who has defended
the nation with his body and his blood is considered ‏is considered‏ at
least as quickly and as completely as the welfare of the 'patriot' who
cries to high heaven his desire to defend the integrity of the American
dollar⸗his own first.

Let us here today say to our heroic dead of all times :
                        you.
'We have not forgotten. We are still the Nation you gave so much to
perpetuate and with the help of Almighty God we make solemn pledge that
this is ‏kttiv‏ still a government of the people, by the people, ‏xhxbxbxb‏
IS for the people, and that this principle shall not perish from the
earth.'

Discovering America (1939)

  For the past three months I have been exploring in these United States and getting acquainted with my fellow Americans.

  Before October 1st, 1931, when I retired from the Marine Corps, I knew something of Philadelphia, Washington and New York on the East coast, considerable about my native State of Pennsylvania and something of the West coast cities. I knew -- from my schooldays -- that there are forty-eight states in our Union, that Canada is to our North and Mexico and the Gulf of Mexico to our South. I knew the names of all -- or nearly all -- the States and of most of the principal cities. Some of the latter I had passed through on trains on several coast-to-coast journeys. Of the people, their hopes and aspirations, their opinions and beliefs, I knew very little.

In fact, while I could easily qualify as a tourist guide in
Mexico City, I didn't know the south side from the Loop in Chicago and
didn't know whether Michigan Boulevard housed the mansions of the ultra-
wealthy or the gambling dives of Al Capone et al. I knew more about the
Island of Haiti, its people and its life, than I did about the smaller
island of Manhattan, a hundred miles from my place of birth, and its teem-
ing millions. I was more familiar with the geography of France and China,
than of the Great Northwest or the State of Michigan.

I knew more of the habits, likes and dislikes of Nicaraguans
and Panamaians than I did of my own people in the South, in the mid-West
or in New England.

I was, in fact, a stranger to my native land and to my fellow
citizens.

But I am getting about and learning.

I am in the midst of a tour of exploration -- a sort of "seeing
America last" tour. I am traveling East and West, North and South, visiting
state capitals and villages, towns and boroughs, metropolises and way-
stations. Between October 1st and December 22nd I traveled some 30,000
miles by rail, plane, bus and motor. I visited 27 states and 62 cities --
keeping my eyes and ears open all the time. Before my present trip ends
in the spring, I will have visited forty of our forty-eight states and
over 100 cities.

Leaving Quantico, Virginia, on October 1st, with my retirement
papers in one pocket and a lecture contract in the other, and wearing
civilian clothes as a regular thing for the first time since 1898, I visited,
in the order named, the following cities:

Greeley, Colorado; Laramie, Wyoming; Salt Lake City and Ogden, Utah; Denver, Colorado Springs, Colorado; Albequerque, New Mexico; Long Beach, Claremont, Los Angeles, Fresno, Oakland, Santa Rosa, San Francisco, California; Portland, Oregon; Seattle, Yakima, Spokane, Washington; Lewiston, Idaho; Pullman, Washington; Butte, Montana; Valley City and Fargo, North Dakota; Minneapolis, Minnesota; Danville, Illinois; Detroit, Michigan; Dayton, Ohio; St. Cloud, Minnesota; Aberdeen, Brookings and Sioux Falls, South Dakota; Omaha, Nebraska; Marshalltown, Iowa; Mansfield, Columbus, Ohio; Huntington, West Virginia; Sandusky and Akron, Ohio; Nashville, Tennessee; Orlando, Gainsville, Jacksonville, Sarasota and Lakeland, Florida; Chicago and Rockford, Illinois; Duluth, Minnesota; Milwaukee, Wisconsin; Chicago; St. Louis and Kansas City in Missouri; Bloomington, Indianapolis, Fort Wayne and Elkhart, Indiana; Cincinnati and Cleveland, Ohio; Syracuse, Gloversville, New York; Boston, Springfield, Massachusetts; Hartford, Connecticut, and Waltham, Massachusetts.

In these cities and towns I made sixty talks and, in addition, spoke briefly at numberless breakfasts, luncheons, dedications, openings and whatnots, to a total of approximately 60,000 men and women.

The lecture business is the reason for this long and continuous hopping about, with virtually every night spent in a Pullman sleeper, but in the course of my skipping hither and yon, with a total disregard of state boundary lines, I am holding long conversations with all sorts of people, and it is these "interviews" that started my education of the United States of 1931 and are continuing it in 1932.

The number of my transient "teachers" totals close to 1500 and their classrooms have been Pullmans, hotel rooms, breakfast, luncheon and dinner tables, motor cars, hotel lobbys and train vestibules.

These "teachers" consist of manufacturers and newspapermen, college professors and train conductors, chiefs of police and salesmen, merchants and lawyers, physicians and Chamber of Commerce officials, chauffeurs and bankers, engineers and hotelmen. They are men and women; wealthy, of moderate circumstance and victims of the depression; they are Republicans, Democrats, Independents and those disgusted with all parties. Many of them are public officials -- Senators, Governors, mayors, councilmen and other office-holders and all the way down to dogcatchers. The 1500 faculty of mine is a true cross-section of our people the Nation over.

#   #   #

It will not surprise anyone, I am sure, that the chief topic of conversation I encountered everywhere was the present economic condition of our land. It may surprise some, however, that our people, while deeply concerned about the problem, are not fearful of the future. I never have had the reputation of being a "Pollyanna" and certainly I have not been one of those super-optimists who, since November, 1929, has peered out of an office window to see prosperity come striding down the street at a rapid gait, ready to turn the corner. However, gloom dispensers in these United States today are few and far between, or else they successfully avoided me. Our people are concerned, of course, about the depression and its consequences. They are concerned for themselves and for their loved ones and equally for those unfortunates whose means of livelihood have been taken from them through no fault of their own.

Long ago I learned that the American people are always kind and helpful to those weaker than themselves, and today they are proving it. Private charity is doing its utmost to care for the unemployed and the other needy. Never before in the history of our land -- not even in war -- has such a demand been made upon the people to aid their own, and never before in the history of any land has a response been so unanimous and so generous. Every city and town I visited has organized its groups, has raised funds and is taking care of its own.

How long the people themselves can take care of the ever growing problem is another matter.

The American people -- with exceptions, naturally -- are not criticising, not whining, not deploring. They realize that the depression is here and they know crying won't help. They are, however, thinking about the situation, wondering what can be the trouble, trying to determine where lies the fault and asking questions of themselves and of others, seeking to learn what can be done.

I have no intention to set myself up as an economist, or an expert on "How to End the Depression." I don't know. No one seems to know -- not even the Department of Commerce of our Government -- but the 1500 collectively have ideas.

It was pointed out to me by bankers, industrialists and others that, in the after-war depression, the automobile business gave us the

necessary impetus to get going. This tremendous industry with its millions
of employees and its vast use of steel, aluminum, copper, rubber, lead,
nickle and gasoline, gave us our great prosperity. Then, when things
slackened up a bit, along came the radio industry with its vast roll of
employees and its tremendous use of raw materials.

Many of my "instructors" are of the opinion that what we need, most
of all, in order that the wheels of industry may start turning once more,
are some new industries. These -- new industries -- plus the injection
of some new lifeblood in some of our major basic industries that seem to
be badly in need of transfusion or major surgery -- are what people seem
to think necessary rather than the cure-alls offered by politicians
and quack doctors.

For instance, in the way of new industries -- the people in South North
Dakota, hard hit by agricultural difficulties, feel that the aluminum deposits there should be mined. These deposits, I was informed there, are of
sufficient quantity to supply all the needs of the United States, which
now imports most of its aluminum, I was told. These people cannot understand why this aluminum is permitted to go unmined. It was pointed out
to me that since the normal industry of the state is "all shot," aluminum
mining would provide a new industry and employment for the people of that
state and for thousands of others who would be attracted thereto.

It is far better to bring an industry to a people than to have a
people migrate to all parts in search of employment.

There is a general feeling, among all classes, that our industrial
organization is in need of modernization as a result of its natural, but
haphazard growth through generations. New England, for instance, needs new

industries to replace those that have diminished in importance or moved to
other sections. New industries are required in the coal producing areas,
where thousands upon thousands of miners are jobless and likely to remain
so in their own industry.

The new blood that some of our industries requires is of various
types. For instance:

In Oregon and Washington, where the lumber mills are idle, they
think the wheels would be started turning by prohibiting the importation
of lumber which, I was informed, comes in a steady stream from abroad.

Steel men in western Pennsylvania and Ohio think that this industry would be revived if steel from Europe could be so taxed that the
foreign manufacturers could not put steel down in New England at less per
ton than our own manufacturers can do in the same place.

Shoe manufacuers see employment for thousands upon thousands if
we can develop here methods of tanning and dyeing leather. Most of our
leather now, I was informed by these people, is shipped abroad to be
tanned and dyed, and then shipped back here to be made into shoes. This
not only adds to the cost of the finished product, but takes away that
much employment.

I learned from my Faculty that our people are not at all radically
inclined. We are a conservative people, with progressive tendencies. The
only radical among the 1500 was a banker in Salt Lake City, and he was
radical in theory only.

I learned that the average American is convinced that no change
in the form of our Government is necessary, or advisable.

The average American, however, seems to think that occasional changes in the personnel of the governing bodies is desirable.

I gathered in my interviews that Americans prefer a politician
to a business man in the responsible executive positions of our Government. They want a man who is extremely human and (seemingly of secondary
importance) able and honest. They prefer a man who will do "favors."
They don't seem to care very much for the strict, business administration
of government.

The general impression throughout the Country is that a change
in National administration is desirable.

The cost of governments, Federal, State and municipal, should be
cut down, the people believe. The cost has crept up in the past ten
years, due to the desire of politicians to maintain their organizations
and thus their power, at the expense of the taxpayer, by adding useless
employees and building unnecessary things in a most extravagant manner.

Very few feel, however, that large numbers of public employees
should be discharged at this time. The weeding-out process should be a
slow one; vacancies should not be filled when they occur.

There is a very general and very noticeable stirring up among all
classes in the matter of interest in public affairs and the deplorable
financial condition of Philadelphia, New York and Chicago, many believe,
is likely to spell the finish of gang rule.

Shortly after I started my tour, there was forwarded to me from
my home a letter from a man who had served in the Cabinet of one of our
Presidents. He wrote:

"If one were to call for a new alignment, asking all those in

favor of giving every American producer from farm and forest,
mill and mine a good faith preference over all the rest of
the world in the market he makes, supports, defends with
his life and is equipped, in part to supply, to step on
one side of the line, while all those who are opposed to giving
any American any preference in any American market, to get
on the other side, you would be surprised, I think. The
country is getting tired of internationalism. The inter-
nationalist has a heart so big that he can love all the
world except an American workman."

That ex-Cabinet member sensed the feeling of the American public.
At least, my conversations with the 1500 seem to confirm his expressed
belief.

I learned that the average American has come to the conclusion
that the best thing for our land is to go back to the old fundamental
rule of:

"America for Americans."

The average American seems to think our Government and a good many
of our people are more concerned over European affairs than those of our
own land. They cannot quite understand why official Washington "falls all
over itself" to greet the emissaries of the European nations who have come
here in the recent past. Everyone seems to think that the visits were made,
not to cement our present friendships, but rather to "get something" out of
America, which seems to be the only country which has anything to give.

Nor can the average American quite understand, despite the explanations and expostulations of our so-called economic experts, why it is good business for the United States to declare a moratorium of war debts to help the European nations and why a similar moratorium to save the farms for the farmers and the homes for the workers who are unable to meet their interest on their mortgages is not as good economics.

As a matter of fact, the average American thinks that neither is good economics.

The opinion prevails, everywhere, that the moratorium is merely the first step. Further postponement of payment, they believe, is in order -- then will come scaling down of debts and, finally, cancellation, with the American business man and farmer and wage-earner all bearing the burden of the tremendous war debt, and it will be up to the Americans to make up the treasury deficit by heavier taxation, just as we will have to do this year to make up the deficit caused by the first moratorium.

Americans, as I encountered them on this tour, are not inclined to approve the giving or leaning of anything to European nations (privately or publicly) until they stop this warring and war operations.

As far as the League of Nations and the World Court are concerned -- they seem to be academic questions with a few college professors, a few publicists and a few statesmen the only ones interested and the only ones knowing anything about them. The average American sees no reason why we should go into the World Court or the League of Nations, and if you ask anyone "Why not?" they point to the fact that Japan thumbed its nose at the entire League and got away with it!

The vast majority is against European entanglements of any kind.

The general impression is that we will require a lot more civilizing before we will agree to submit vital questions, matters of life and death, to a jury of Russians, Turks, Japanese and Rumanians.

I have not found one man who would submit a question of ownership of his home to a decision of Mexicans, Nicaraguans and Haitiens. All are in favor of peace, but it is just a question of procedure to secure it.

Prohibition, it seems, has lost its big kick as a controversial subject for the time being, at least. Of course, the organized "Wets" and "drys" are doing their best to keep the issue alive. There also seems to be a growing feeling that no matter what we do about it, conditions will not improve very much and that there won't be any less drinking, regardless of what is said or done. Most people are of the opinion that Prohibition has brought evils as great as those of liquor itself, and most of them are tired of what they call the constant parading of dishonesty in public office -- they mean that there is too much graft connected with the enforcement of liquor laws and that liquor is too easily obtainable at any rate. But they feel that something should be done about it.

#   #   #

As I look back over the first three months of this tour, and as I continue trotting about the country, scheduled to visit 13 additional states and more than two score additional cities, I am beginning to realize that the men who make up the Marine Corps, and the Army and Navy as well -- the men with whom I have served all my life -- are just like the Americans I am meeting on this trip. How could it be otherwise? I realize now they are the same flesh and blood as those who till the soil, who work at lathes

in factories, who stand behind the counters in mercantile establishments
and in counting houses, who manufacture shoes or sell bonds. They are all
Americans.

I found that the people in mufti have just as high regard for
the men in uniform now as they had in wartime. I read of disarmament conferences and of peace and pacifism, but the American people still believe in an
adequate Army and Navy -- possibly more so today than ever before.

The American public has been most kind to me on this, my initial
venture into a new field, and in every city I have visited I have been met
at the train by a committee headed, almost without exception, by the mayor
of the city and the chief of police -- all policemen seem to think of me as
one of them since my experience in Philadelphia, and I am extremely proud
of this distinction.

In nearly every city I have been met at the station also by
officers of the regular Army, Reserves and National Guard, and, on several
occasions, by Army bands from nearby posts which, in every instance,
played "Sweet Adeline," my favorite tune. The Army has been most polite
and kind to me and I am very grateful. I have seen very few Naval officers
on my tour. Ex-Marines, of course, have met me at every stop and have been
most affectionate.

NOTE: The opinions or assertions contained herein are
private ones of the writer and are not to be construed as
official or reflecting the views of the Navy Department
or the Naval Service at large.

The War in Europe (Undated)

General Butler – Radio – 1　　　*getting it up*

Thank you, Senator ~~and~~ Clark.

My fellow Americans, let's look at this European war.

Let's see if we should be all hot and bothered over it.
Did we have anything to do with it? You know we didn't---and
I know we didn't! And I'll tell you why.

We didn't have one single, solitary thing to do with any
of the crooked, back-alley maneuvering that brought this war
into existence.

We weren't present at its birth. We weren't consulted about
the doctor. We didn't even meet the nurse.

Now, that being the case, are we going to be dumb enough to
let ~~them~~ leave it on our doorstep?

Are we going to let them say: "Here it is! It's yours, too.
~~And~~ you feed it!"

There may be a lot of shooting going on over in Europe, but
there's an awful lot of sound and fury going on over here.

Don't let them kid us. Keep your eye on one thing.
The way to get into this war is to raise the embargo on arms.

Remember that one thing. It's the heart and soul of the
matter. If you want to be dragged in, just start selling arms and
munitions.

Nations are like people you know. Some try to lead honorable
lives. Some are untrustworthy. Some are like rats.

But what would you say if a couple of fellows started a terrific
scrap down the street, and somebody came running up to you and said:
"Want to get into that scrap?" You'd say: "No! It isn't my scrap.
I want to be neutral." And then, this well-meaning guy would say:

Revise---2.

"Swell! ~~Here's~~ [*Here's*] a pile of rocks, brickbats, and clubs. Hand them
out to one ~~or the other~~ of those ~~fellows scrapping~~ [*sluggers*], or even both of
them. ~~and~~ [*T*]hat's the way to keep neutral."

Now, in the case of ~~a couple of individual battlers~~, what would
you think if anybody gave you that kind of advice?

I don't even have to tell you.

Now, getting back to the mess on the other side of the Atlantic,
~~~~, here's one of the ways they're using to ~~drag~~ try to drag us
in.

They say, well, if the British and the French don't lick Hitler,
Hitler will be over here and on our necks.

He'll be bombing our women and children and shelling our cities.

Don't let anybody feed you that misinformation.

It doesn't take a military education to figure out what I'm
going to tell you.

It will take not less than one million soldiers to invade the
United States with any hope of ~~~~ [*even getting ashore.*]
~~These million men must come all at once.~~

They must bring not less than seven tons of ~~~~ [*baggage*] per man.
One million men, seven million tons of ~~~~ ~~~~, ammunition, what-not.

They must bring four hundred thousand motor vehicles. They've
got to find room for fifty gallons of gasoline per day for each
vehicle for 270 days--that's nine months' supply.

Why, the[*re are*]~~'re~~ not enough ships in the whole world to carry that
kind of an expedition. And remember, those ships have ~~got~~ to ~~~~ [*have*]
enough fuel to get back with--to make the round trip.

[handwritten top right: This scraps down the street]

Revise---3.

Any dumb cluck can see that.

But here's some more: they've got to have harbors to land in. Docks to get their stores ashore. You know, you can't stop 25 miles out at sea, drop a 50-ton armored tank overboard, and tell it to swim ashore and meet you on Broadway.

You know very well we're not going to open our ~~harbor~~ harbors to them, prepare docks for them, and invite them in.

New York harbor is the only big one we have on this coast
                    all you have to do
and to block New York harbor/is to dump two days' garbage in ~~the~~ *THE CHANNEL* instead of hauling it out to sea.

~~Even if we had no support, Navy, and we've gotta buddy, one,~~

~~They couldn't come everywhere.~~

And don't forget that we happen to have a Navy and it's the best in the world.

Now, what about an aerial invasion?

Well, Colonel Lindbergh and Eddie Rickenbacher, the two foremost fliers we have, already have told you it's ridiculous to talk or ~~to~~ think about bombing New York from Berlin.

And don't forget that we have an air force of our own.

So, my fellow Americans, let's take one thing at a time.

This war's in Europe. It isn't over here. And it won't come over here unless we invite it. But the way to invite it is to sell bombs and munitions. They'll have the stamp of American makers on them and they'll have the R. S. V. P. that'll bring about acceptance of ~~an~~ *That* invitation. *AN INVITATION TO GO OVER THERE AND JOIN IN THE MESS. OH, BUT THE BOOGEY BOO IS THAT SOMEBODY WILL COME.* Don't be alarmed. Nobody in Europe can afford to leave home. Why, if Hitler leaves Germany with a million soldiers to come over here, if he ever got back he'd find everybody speaking either French *or*

Revise---4.

Russian. Those babies would move in on him while he was gone.

No, there isn't a single crazy war dog that can come over here. We can build a defense of our own country that not even a rat, let alone a mad dog, could creep through.

But let's be consistent. We cry to high Heaven that we are a Christian and a peace-loving nation. We don't believe in shooting people, bombing their homes, knocking down their cities with cannon. We really are a Christian, peace-loving people, but I say to you it's unChristian, hypocritical and unmanly to say to the British and the French--"We're against this fellow, Hitler, and being Christian and peace-loving we can't shoot him, we can't bomb him, but we'll be delighted to see you do it, and we'll furnish the guns and the bombs. That is, providing you pay us double what they're worth. And in order there may be no mistake this time--you'll pay in advance!

How often are we going over there to bail out Europe? Will we have to do it every 25 years? In addition to sending our children today, are we going to be ready to send our grandchildren 25 years from now?

Are we so much interested right now that we want to contribute five million of the finest and the strongest boys that the great mothers of America have produced?

Are you mothers and fathers so deeply interested that you want to furnish your sons?

Well--start selling ammunition and that's what you'll have to do.

Don't you realize the money you get for your ammunition will be covered with blood? And, as time goes on,

Revise---5.

this blood will be the blood of your own children.

Has blood money ever brought anything but misery to those who got the money?

Look what happened to the billions of dollars we made out of the last war.

It brought us a situation where even today--twenty years later-- there are ten million of us out of work.

And if we allow ourselves to handle any more of this stinking blood money there'll be twenty million of us out of work--~~~~~~~~ maybe for ~~~~~~~~~~~~~~~ the next fifty years.

But that isn't all. Let's get back to cases, and look at this thing from a personal viewpoint.

It's all very well and high-sounding to say that ~~a~~ the Government ~~To say we~~ have nothing to do with it. declares war. We enter the war--but who are we? Well, "we", right now, are the mothers and fathers of every able-bodied boy of military age in the United States. "We" are also you young men of voting age and ~~over they'll use for cannon fodder.~~

Now--you Mothers, particularly!

The only way you can resist all this war hysteria and beating of tom-toms is by asserting the love you bear your boys. When you listen to some well worded, some well-delivered war speech, just remember it's nothing but sound. I tell you that no amount of sound can make up to you for the loss of your boy. After you've heard one of those speeches and your blood's all hot and you want to bite somebody~~like Hitler--go upstairs where your boy's asleep.

Go into his bedroom. You'll find him lying there, pillow all messed up, covers all tangled, sleeping away so hard. Look at him. Put your hand on that spot on the back of his neck--the place you

Revise---6.

used to love to kiss when he was a tiny baby. Just rub it a little.
You won't wake him up. Just look at his strong, fine young body
because only the best boys are chosen for war. Look at this splendid
young creature who's part of yourself, then close your eyes for
a moment and I'll tell you what can happen.

       actually

You won't see it, but I have seen it, and I can describe it
to you. You can imagine it.

     But first, you have a fifty-fifty chance of never seeing your
boy again if you let this embargo on arms be raised and your boy
is conscripted and sent overseas to fight.

     If you ever do see him again, fifty times out of a hundred he'll
be a maimed and helpless cripple all his life.

     Why, you say, that can't happen. That wasn't true in the last
war. But the last European war saw us fighting just about
150 days and we had more than a quarter of a million casualities.
Try to get out of this war inside of fifteen hundred days!

get this picture of your boy while you're standing there
in the dark of the bedroom where he's peacefully sleeping--trusting
you.

     That boy relies on you. You brought him into this world. You
cared for him. Now, I ask you: Are you going to run out on him?
Are you going to let someone beat a drum or blow a bugle and make
him run after it? Thank God, this is a Democracy and by your voice
and your vote you can save your boy. You are the bosses of this
country--you mothers, you fathers.

     And now for that other picture I said I'd give you. That other
picture that can be the picture of your boy.

     Somewhere--five thousand miles from home. Night. Darkness.
Cold. A drizzling rain. The noise is terrific. All Hell has broken
loose.

V--Revise.

A star shell bursts in the air. Its unearthly magic flare lights
up the muddy field. There's a lot of tangled wires out there and
RUSTY BARBED
a boy hanging over them--his stomach ripped out, feebly calling
AND HE'S
for help and water. His lips are set tight. He's in agony.

There's your boy. The same boy lying in bed tonight. The
same boy who trusts you. Do you want him to be the next unknown
soldier? The last one had a mother. And a father. He just didn't
appear.

And listen: you mothers and fathers. I've had the heart-rending
experience in my time of sitting with some of your sons as they've
gone over. I've listened to the pathetic little last messages they've
wanted carried back to you. I've accepted and delivered the poor
little keepsakes they've wanted you to have.

Do you want your boy, tangled in barbed wire, struggling for
or
a last gasp of breath in stinking trenches somewhere abroad,
do you want him to cry out: "Oh, Mother--Oh, Father...why did you
let them do it?"

Think it over, my dear fellow Americans. Think if all this is
worth it.

Can't we be satisfied with defending our own homes--our own women,
our own children?

There are only two reasons why you should ever be asked to give
your youngsters.

One is the defense of our homes. The other is the defense of
the bill of rights--and particularly the right to worship God as we
see fit.

Every other reason advanced for the murder of our young men is
a racket pure and simple.

Revise---8.

And yet if you sit still and allow this thing to ~~die~~ go on;
if you allow this hysteria to mount, this propaganda to take hold
of you; if you allow this embargo on arms to be raised; if you allow
our national pockets to jingle with blood money, I tell you that
you can prepare to say goodbye to your boy.

I beg you, don't ~~them~~ let them do this! I beg of you to sit
down <u>this</u> <u>very</u> <u>minute</u> and write a message to your congressman, and
your senator or to our president.

That's your right--your constitutional right, *OF APPEAL.* That's your
privilege.

Kepp this arms embargo on tight! ~~Keep them from xxxxx dotting~~
~~those perpetual war-torn fields of Europe with the bodies of our~~
~~American boys. Good night.~~

THEY'VE BEEN FIGHTING FOR A THOUSAND
YEARS IN EUROPE; SINCE THE DAWN OF
HISTORY REALLY. DON'T LET THEM DOT
THOSE BLOOD-DRENCHED FIELDS WITH THE
BODIES OF OUR AMERICAN BOYS.

GOOD NIGHT.

Avoiding War in the Pacific
by Attending to Our Own Business (1939)

While my subject is "Avoiding War in the Pacific," it is felt that the American people are vitally interested in avoiding wars in all oceans and in all lands.

A practicable and workable technique to avoid wars in which the United States may become involved is not limited in its application to the Pacific Ocean and will work equally well in the Atlantic Ocean or the Black Sea—if those who work it are unselfish and honest.

If wars are to be avoided by our country it can be done only by determined and simple political action on the part of the great majority of our people—the trusting majority—which majority does not get up the wars, but which does fight them and which does pay all the bills in blood and money. So it is this great majority to which these words are addressed, in an effort to awaken their interest.

This great majority has neither the time nor the inclination to study the so-called economic causes of war; this majority is interested only in keeping out of wars of all kinds. This majority is not vitally interested in the means by which we are kept out of war. You must remember—wars do not just occur—they are made by men. All efforts which keep us out will be approved, and there will never be a Congressional investigation into the steps taken or the methods adopted, which saved us from a war. There would be nothing to investigate. Men who took a part in peace would be only too willing to publish to the world all their moves.

Editor's Note: Page two of this document was unavailable and is not included.

...bones—"to make the world safe for Democracy"—"I went fighting the business of wars." Rot—pure, unadulterated, sickening rot. (…) saying of their lives and their (…) which led those (…) die and are (…) on the (…) left behind (…) those whose financial condition would benefit (…) to lose.

Appealing peace slogans must be coined and there could be nothing more potent than, "Attend to our own business."

Then the question is—"What is our own business?" To answer that we must first decide what is meant by that word "Our." I contend that "Our," where war is concerned, refers to the people who do the fighting—those who make the sacrifices in blood and never-ending sorrow. I contend that the business of these people is the preservation and protection only of their lives and their homes. Certainly those who die and are maimed on the field of battle and those left behind to sorrow to the of their days cannot, by any stretch, claim an interest in foreign investments.

Our trade with Japan and China together in 1936 showed a balance of about five million dollars in our favor—about one-twelfth the cost of a battleship—and how many of those who might bleed would share in that five millions? We exported to China and Japan 251 millions of dollars worth of products in 1936 and imported 246 millions of dollars worth of their goods. There is nothing we must have from the East in order to live—and live happily and comfortably too. Of course it is desirable—highly desirable to have trade and friendly relations with the Far East.

It is also highly desirable to have amicable relations with the grocer but it certainly will not promote friendly relations if you keep standing in front of his store with a gun. The grocer, or the coal dealer, will not object to a man keeping a gun in his own front yard to protect his home—nor will he object to his keeping fierce watch dogs in his yard to protect him and his family from marauders—but he has every right to vigorously object and even be suspicious of his neighbour's friendly intentions if the neighbor insists on stationing savage watch dogs in front of his store. No, it is not neighborly, nor is it common sense to so maneuver as to force the owner of property to turn it over to you without just payment.

If a nation's reputation for fair dealing is good that nation can always get, by purchase, what it needs.

Now what do we mean by this phrase "Own Business." It does not necessarily refer to trade—in this instance it more properly refers to conduct. So we have "attend to our own conduct.'

Which means: take only a friendly, helpful part in the affairs of others—spread no slander about others—make no faces at others with our Navy—keep our Navel manoeuvres at home—treat all nations alike.

Put all nations on a quota footing with respect to immigration—put our own foreign relations house in order. Tell the whole world just what we intend to defend with our armed forces. Let the world know that we do not intend to invade them or seize their property and that our armed forces are so designed that we could not invade even if a change of administration should cause a change of policy. This would set a fine example and establish us as a square-dealing nation. Then let us make publicly the necessary preparations to carry out our published policy.

In conclusion: when we announced what we intend to defend let us put our national flag over it and forbid the flying of our flag over anything else. Then we will banish our most usual and popular cause for our wars. Our flag belongs to all of us Americans and we Americans should have a voice in where it is flown.

Concerning Law Enforcement
(Undated)

Thank you, —

My fellow Americans:

Let's look over this European brawl and see where we stand.

Let's see if we have contributed one single thing to cause it.

Let's see if even a part of the responsibility can be pinned on us.

Let's see if we have anything at all to do with it.

If we think it over calmly, we all know perfectly well that we did not have one solitary blessed thing to do with the making of this mess over there.

Did we have anything to do with any promises Britain and France made to Poland? No, we didn't.

Did we have anything to do with Hitler's land grabbing? No, we didn't.

Did we have anything to do with Britain and France declaring war on Germany? We certainly did not and were not even consulted.

These are the SMELLY things in this pit of European back-alley politics into which we will be pushed if we don't watch our step—if we are fools enough to raise the embargo on the sale of arms to these war-mad European politicians, if we are naive enough to allow ourselves to get all excited about this brawl that is going on over there, as brawls have, almost since the dawn of history.

Before they started this row over land and natural resources, did they ask our advice—much less our encouragement?

No, they did not, and we neither advised nor encouraged them, so why should we get all stewed up about it.

Just because people on the other side of the world insist on continuing their age-old practise of committing mass suicide, do we as a nation have to follow their example and blow out our brains too.

Are we to adopt a policy of sitting around this European cockpit and going to the rescue of our favorite cocks whenever they get into a fight they might not be able to win without us?

Are we to become so entangled in European high pressure politics that the main issue at our elections will be whether or not to allow political changes abroad?

If we are to make it our practise to take part in these cock-fights over there we should certainly vote on it—have it in all our national political platforms.

Twenty-five years ago we went abroad to bail out Britain and France, helped drench the gore-sodden fields of Europe with the blood of a quarter million of our finest boys—the pride of our manhood—helped sow the seeds of the present orgy—spent fifty billion dollars on that adventure.

But are WE to blame because Hitler built himself a great hair trigger war machine?

Are WE responsible that England and France did not build a machine to stop him?

Are WE culpable in any way because Hitler started before the other side was ready?

Provided Britain and France really want to stop Hitler, are WE to make up for their failure to prepare to do so by sticking out OUR necks and raising our embargo on arms?

Suppose you are walking down a strange street in a strange town in a strange country thousands of miles from your own home. You come across a brawl. You have no interest in it except that it is a fight. All of a sudden you hear one of the brawlers cry out in your native tongue as he swats his opponent: "I believe in Democracy." You don't know in the least what the fight is about but your sympathies are with the fellow who speaks your language. The believer in Democracy sees you and shout: "Come on and get in—we believe in the same things, and if he wins you'll be next, what's more."

You reply, "No, I don't want to. I'm a stranger and don't want to get mixed up in this. I like you but not enough to get into a fight over it."

"All right," he says, "you gather up all the clubs, stones and brickbats you can get hold of and feed them to me, I'LL use them on the other fellow."

Do you really thing that if you start handing your Democratic friend ammunition, you won't get into it too? You can't help it, if he's losing, and if he wins, he will surely call you a scab, say he could have won by himself anyhow, and declare he owe you nothing.

On the other hand if you stay out of his fight, with which you had nothing to do in the first place, the argument that if the other fellow wins, he will give YOU a good beating too, won't apply. You will have gone about your business, instead of butting into a fight into which you did not belong, and the winner won't find you right there ready to be chewed up next.

They say—well, if the French and British don't lick Hitler, he will be over here and jump on our necks next. He'll be bombing our women and children and shelling our cities.

Don't let anybody feed you that rot. It doesn't take military education to figure out what I am going to tell you:

It will take NOT LESS THAN ONE MILLION soldiers to invade the United States with any hope of getting ashore. These million men must come all at once. They must bring not less than SEVEN MILLION TONS OF BAGGAGE per man. One million men, seven tons of food, ammunition, whatnot.

For instance, just one item: They must bring four hundred thousand vehicles alone, tractors, trucks, tanks and the like. They've got to find room for fifty gallons of gasoline per day for each vehicle for 270 days—that's nine months' supply. Why there are not enough ships in the whole world, including our own—and we certainly wouldn't lend them outs—to carry that kind of an expedition. And remember these ships have to bring with them enough fuel to get back with—to make the round trips. We certainly aren't going to give them fuel over here to go home with. Any dumb cluck can see that.

But here's some more. They've got to have harbors to land in, docks to get their stores ashore. You know you can't stop twenty-five miles out at sea, drop a fifty ton armored tank overboard and tell it to swim ashore and meet you on Broadway. Remember, that with all the harbors, docks and ships of England and France at our disposal in the World War it took us nineteen months to get

1,900,000 men to France. And that though this expedition was headed for a friendly country and all possible help on the other side was ours, it took months of preparation after the United States had actually declared war before it was safe to send the actual troops over.

You know very well WE aren't going to open our harbors to them, prepare docks for them and invite them in. New York Harbor is the only big one we have on this coast and to block New York Harbor all you have to do is to dump two days' garbage in the channel, instead of hauling it out to sea.

Don't you see, it's all a question of supply—this invading business. Men and munitions, but chiefly munitions. Seems that munitions always run out before the supply of man is exhausted.

Just figure it out for yourselves: For every man at the front you must start out from your home depots with a thousand lbs. of supplies: food, ammunition, gasoline, clothing, medical supplies, engineering supplies, spare parts etc. to say nothing of replacements of the above.

You must also send off for every day of his absence half a ton of stuff per man at the front.

Remember also that for every thousand miles you go across water on an invading expedition into a hostile land you must take ninety days' stores of all kinds. It is over 3,000 miles across the Atlantic—three times ninety is two hundred and seventy days—nine months. No, the supply of an European Army is out of the question—that is a Army big enough to land here.

There is another thing to remember: No fleet can operate more than 1500 miles from its base and Germany proper would be the base of a Hitler invading fleet. No he couldn't get his fleet over here, or get it home again.

But—they say—he might build a BASE somewhere in South America. Well, my friends, those who got up that little idea overlooked the fact that it is further by a good deal from Berlin to South America than from Berlin to New York, so that the difficulties of transport would be immeasurably more complicated than they already are anyhow. And when he got to South America, he would be a good deal further away from us, than if he had come straight over from Berlin. So don't let that frighten you. It is all pure propaganda and insane at that to talk of Hitler invading us.

And don't forget, that we happen to have a Navy and it's the best in the world too.

Now, what about an serial invasion? Well,—Colonel Lindbergh and Eddie Rickenbacher, the two foremost fliers we have, already have told us it's ridiculous to talk of an invasion by air or to talk or think about bombing New York from Berlin.

But suppose they do invent a plane that might be able to do it. That airplane has got to make the round trip too. And without landing. With the fuel with which it started. And even if they achieve a plane that will do that we have enough brains in this country to make some sort of machine that will destroy it before it hurts our woman and children.

And don't forget we have an air force of our own, and a fine one too.

So let's take one thing at a time.

This war's in Europe, it isn't over here. And it won't come over here unless we invite it. And the last way to invite it is to raise this embargo and sell bombs and ammunitions. They'll have the stamp of American makers on them and they'll have the R.S.V.P. that will bring about that invitation. An invitation to go over there and join in the mess.

Oh but the bogey boo is that someone will come over here. Don't be alarmed. No one in Europe can afford to leave home. Why, if Hitler were to leave Germany with a million man to go anywhere, if he ever got back he'd find everybody speaking French or Russian. These babies would move in on him while he was gone.

No, there isn't a single crazy war dog than can come over here. We can build a defense of our own country that not even a rat, much less a mad dog could creep through.

Let's be consistent. We cry to high Heaven that we are a Christian and peace loving nation and therefore we don't believe in shooting people, bombing their homes, knocking down their cities with cannon.

And we really ARE a Christian and peace-loving people, and therefore it's unchristian, hypocritical and commonly of us to say to the British and the French: "Sure, we're against this fellow Hitler, but being Christian, WE can't shoot him, WE can't bomb him, but we'll be delighted to see YOU do it, and we'll furnish the guns and the bombs. That is provided you pay us double what they're worth. And in order that there may be no mistake about it this time, you'll pay us in advance.

"You see we're against going to war ourselves, but we're not against YOUR wars. You go ahead. We'll sell you the stuff."

But make no mistake about it. The time has come when we have got to answer the Big Question before us, and here it is:

How often are we going over there to bail out Europe? Will we have to do it every twenty-five years?

In addition to going ourselves last time, are we going to send our children today, are we going to be ready to send our grand-children twenty five years from now? Isn't it time to make a stand about this thing here and now?

Are we so much interested right now that we want to con-tribute five million of the finest and strongest boys that the great Mothers of America have produced? Are you mothers and fathers so deeply interested that you want to furnish your sons? Well,—start selling them ammunition, and that's what you'll have to do.

Don't you realize that the money you'll get for your ammuni-tion will be covered with blood? And as time goes on this blood will be the blood of your children.

Has blood money ever brought anything but misery to those who got that money?

Look what happened to the billions of dollars we made out of the last war: It brought us a situation where even today—twenty years later—there are ten millions of us out of work. And if we allow ourselves to handle any more of this stinking blood money, there'll be twenty millions of us out of work—maybe for the next fifty years.

But that isn't all. Let's go back to cases and look at this thing from a personal view point, which is the only one that counts in the long run: It's all very well and high sounding to say: The Government declares war. To say helplessly: as individuals we have nothing to do with it, can't prevent it.

But WHO ARE "WE"?

Well, "we" right now are the mothers and fathers of every ablebodied boy of military age in the United States. "We" are also you young man of voting age and over, that they'll use for cannon fodder. And "we" CAN prevent it.

Now—YOU MOTHERS, particularly:

The only way you can resist all this war hysteria and beating of tomhoms is by hanging onto the love you bear your boys. When you listen to some well worded, well delivered war speech, just remember it's nothing but sound. It's your boy that matters. And no amount of sound can make up to you for the loss of your Boy.

After you've heard one of those speeches and your blood is all hot and you want to go and bite someone like Hitler—go upstairs where your boy's asleep.

Go into his bedroom. You'll find him lying there, pillows all messed up, covers all tangled, sleeping away so hard. Look at him. Put your hand on that spot at the back of his neck, the place you used to love to kiss when he was a baby. Just stroke it a little. You won't wake him up, he knows it's you. Just look at his strong fine young body—because only the BEST boys are chosen for war. Look at this splendid young creature who's apart of yourself, and then close your eyes for a moment and I'll tell you what can happen. YOU won't actually see it, you won't be there, but I have seen it, and I can describe it to you.

But before I do that I have to remind you that you have a fifty-fifty chance of never seeing your boy again at all, if you let this embargo an arms be raised and your boy is conscripted and sent overseas to fight. And if you ever do see him again, fifty times out of a hundred he'll be a helpless cripple or nervously shot all his life.

Have you ever been for one of those huge Veterans Hospitals it has been necessary to build to take care of the thousands of helpless and maimed cripples still with us from the LAST war?

If you have, you will not need a reminder of what war can do to your boy, how it can render his life useless and broken at twenty, and yet keep him cruelly alive through the whole span of it.

If you have not, I advise you to go and see one of them, for nothing could bring home to you more clearly or tragically the fact that in the last analysis it is your boy who is going to pay the piper. Few there are who come back entirely unsheathed, and some come back in such a way that you would find yourself praying for their release from pain.

Those withered, elderly, spiritless men who lie and sit so patiently in their wards day after day in those hospitals, waiting for the end as they have waited since they got there twenty years ago, weres the flower of our boys in their time. It is not age that has brought them to this pass, for their average age is little over forty, it is war. Like the Unknown Soldier who was one of them, they too had mothers and fathers who felt towards them as you do about your boy.

Now get this picture of your boy, as you stand there in the dark of the bedroom, where has peacefully sleeping—trusting you.

You brought him into the world. You cared for him. That boy relies on you. You taught him to that, didn't you?

Now I ask you: Are you going to run out on him? Are you going to let someone beat a drum or blew a bugle and make him chase after it and get himself killed or crippled in a foreign land?

Thank God, this is a democracy, and by your voice and by your vote you can save your boy. YOU are the bosses of this country—you mothers, you fathers.

And that brings up another point: If you let this country go into a European war you will lose this democracy, don't forget that.

And now for that other picture I said I'd give you, that other picture that could be the picture of your boy, if you let him go abroad to fight. It may help you to build up resistance against all this propaganda which will almost drown you.

Somewhere in a muddy trench, thousands of miles from you and his time your boy, the same one that was sleeping so sweetly and safely in his bed when you watched him in a dead of night—is waiting to "go over the top." Four o'clock in the morning, drizzling rain, dark and dismal, face caked with mad and tears, so so homesick and longing for you and home—thinks of you on your knees praying for him—frightened to death, but still more scared the boy next to him will discover his terror, that's your boy. Stomach as big as an egg, I know, I've had that sensation many times I was sixteen the first time anyone shot at me in Cuba, two thousand miles from my home, waiting the same way…God, the suspense!

Do you want him to be next Unknown Soldier? The Unknown Soldier had a mother, you know, and a father. He didn't just appear out of the air.

Do you want your boy, tangled in the barbed wire, or struggling for a last gasp of breath in a stinking trench somewhere abroad, do you want him to cry out: "Oh Mother, oh, Father, why did you let them do it?"

Think it over my dear fellow Americans.

Can't we be satisfied with defending our own homes, our own women, our own children? Right here in America?

There are only two reasons why you should ever be asked to give your youngsters. One is the defense of our homes. The other is the defense of the Bill of Rights and particularly the right to worship God as we see fit. Every other reason advanced for the murder of young men is a racket, pure and simple.

And yet, if you sit still, and allow this thing to happen, if you allow this hysteria to mount, this propaganda to take hold of you, if you allow our national pockets to jingle with blood money, I tell you that you may as well prepare to say goodbye to your boy.

The meat of this whole American Coconut is the Embargo on Arms. Whether or not we run a real risk of becoming involved depends on whether we keep the lid on the Embargo. We know that if we keep it on we shall have no war profits. If we take it off we may make some money, but it will all be "stage money" and covered with blood to boot.

Keep the arms Embargo on tight: They've been fighting for a thousand years in Europe. Don't let them dot again those blood drenched foreign fields with the bodies of our American boys. Sit down this very minute and write a message to your Congressman, and your Senator, and your President. That's your right—your constitutional right of appeal. It's also your privilege. Right now, I firmly believe it's your duty, if you want to save your boys.

Good night.

Veterans' Rights (Undated)

An Associated Press dispatch from Washington, D.C., on October 23rd stated that less than 40 per cent of those veterans who had been on the compensation rolls in presumptive cases were being retained by the special review boards which have passed on approximately 27,000 cases to date. This means that more than 60 per cent of these disabled and chronically ill veterans have been entirely cut off from government compensation which formerly provided them with the necessities of life, even if it could not restore to them the health and security they sacrificed in their country's service.

What is to happen to these men and their families? Well, there are two things that can happen to them - they can starve or they can become the public charges of organized charity in this city and in every other community of the United States. Understand - the review boards do not say that these veterans are not ill or are not disabled - all they say is that such illness and such disability cannot be proved to have had their origin in service. Of course it cant be proved in a majority of cases. Incomplete or lost records, the fact that the patient himself did not recognize as permanent an ailment or disability he experienced during the war, or many other sound reasons, make it impossible to obtain such proof.

These men and their families - 60 per cent of those who have been receiving a living allowance from the government - now suddenly are reduced to absolute want.

The men are unable to work even if work could be found for them. As a result, it

becomes the duty of this city, and of other cities and towns, to add these men and

their families to the already long lists of depression victims and public charges

which cost the taxpayers of this country untold millions of dollars each year.

The Veterans of Foreign Wars of the United States has formulated a six fold

program as a foundation for all veteran welfare legislation.

. First, we believe the care of the veteran is a federal responsibility to be

paid for out of federal taxes. The bulk of these taxes is paid by those who enjoy

large incomes and those who have profited most through the years of America's

prosperity. It is unfair and un-American in principle to place this burden of cost

upon the local community and upon local charities, where the small taxpayer is

already crushed beneath the burden of heavy taxation.

Adequate relief for veterans suffering from injury or disease incurred in

actual war service is the second of the legislative aims of the V.F.W., while the

third objective is relief for veterans suffering from disabilities due to injury,

disease or old age who are no longer able to be self-supporting. The V.F.W. be-

lieves that the federal government has no moral right to regard the care of these

veterans as a burden that should fall upon the local community.

Fourthly, we demand relief for the widows and orphans of all veterans, regardless

of the cause of the veteran's death. These women and children are entitled to a

chance to live and the matter of their welfare is a responsibility which belongs to

the federal government.

In the fifth place, we do not believe that compensation, pensions or hospital-

ization should be with-held from any veteran or his dependents until they can prove

they are paupers. Such a condition is unfair and un-American and tends to destroy

self-respect. Lastly, the Veterans of Foreign Wars of the United States believes in the

immediate cash payment of the adjusted service certificates, or bonus, not because it

is a favor or special benefit for the veteran - not even because such payment was

acknowledged a just debt by the Congress of the United States several years ago and

a just debt should be settled now, not twelve or fifteen years from now.

We maintain that immediate cash payment of adjusted service certificates would

be a material and effective contribution to America's recovery from the worse economic

depression of history.   In order to assure this recovery, it is necessary that the

purchasing power of the masses must be increased. Immediate payment of the bonus

would distribute to three and one-half million veterans, representing between

twelve and fifteen million individuals, cash amounting to two billion, five hundred million dollars. Such payment would affect the entire country immediately, for the

money would quickly reach the channels of commerce and trade and would create jobs and

stimulate industry and business in general.

We have always regarded the care of our widows and orphans and our disabled

comrades as our first obligation. In this direction we have consistently opposed

piece-meal legislation for veterans and constantly advocated a policy of generosity

and tolerance in their behalf.

As long as there are widows and orphans of veterans and as long as there are

disabled veterans whose lives have been wrecked by the havoc of war, our organization

will continue to dedicate its labors in their behalf. We will accept no compromises!

Will recognize no excuses! As long as there are wars to be fought, and as long as men

must be called upon to abandon homes and loved ones for the purpose of facing the

guns and bayonnets of an enemy, the Veterans of Foreign Wars of the United States

will devote its energies to their well being when these emergencies have passed. We

will never choose the path of submission to those who would abuse the sacred rights of

our disabled comrades. These wrongs against which we stand opposed are no common

wrongs. They out to the very roots of human welfare.

We believe, with the late Calvin Coolidge, that "the pension roll is America's roll of honor." We will fight with every ounce of our energy any movement that seeks to identify America's disabled and needy veterans, or their widows and orphans, as paupers or objects of charity before the government sees fit to assume its proper responsibilities in their behalf. The suggestion that a veteran, who has worn the uniform of the United States government in time of war, must be virtually destitute and a burden upon his community, before the federal government can even take his plight into consideration, is in utter violation of the American spirit of fair play and the traditions of government to which we are already committed. The fact that this government had to summon to its aid more than four and a half million of America's manhood to successfully conduct its operations during the World War, is no fault of the many thousands of veterans who find themselves in need and physically incapacitated today.

We must not forget that there were more men enrolled in the ranks of the Army, Navy and Marine Corps during the World War than in all our previous wars put together. The cost of caring for these men upon their return from the scene of war is a question that we should have carefully deliverated back in the spring of 1917, when public sentiment demanded of Congress that war with Germany be declared. If - today - the cost in dollars for the care of these veterans, and their dependents, seems to some

rather high and out of proportion to other phases of our federal government, there

is truly no occasion for surprise. We are only faced with the costly aftermath

and logical conclusion that must unfortunately follow every conflict between

nations. Even though this cost may seem terrific, we must not forget that the

loss of one's life, his health, or even a limb is something that can never be

replaced through a pension or compensation.

These are the principles that characterize the program and activities of the

Veterans of Foreign Wars of the United States as it exists today. I sincerely

advise the cooperation of all veteran organizations, and all patriotic societies,

in a united movement that will help withstand the attacks of present day anti-

veteran groups. To those veterans who are not giving their individual support to

organized veterandom in this crisis, I urge prompt and consistent affiliation with

some veteran organization. If you are eligible to the ranks of the Veterans of

Foreign Wars of the United States, through overseas service in either the war

with Spain or the World War, or intermittent campaigns and expeditions, we believe

your rightful place is at our side. We offer you this opportunity to be of service -

not only to your disabled comrades and to those who have been unable to rehabilitate themselves since returning to civil life and their dependents - but to your own

loved ones and yourself as well. It is an honor and a distinction to be eligible

to any veteran organization. This is especially true when you can claim membership

under the Cross of Malta in the Veterans of Foreign Wars of the United States.

RADIO ADDRESSES

Address From October 11, 1939

GENERAL BUTLER - 1

Thank you, Mr. Griffin.

My fellow Americans:

Let's look over this European brawl and see where we stand on it or why we should stand anywhere on it for that matter.

First, let's see if we have contributed one single thing to cause it.

Also let's see if even a part of the responsibility for it can be pinned on us.

Finally, let's see if we have anything at all to do with it.

If we think it over calmly, we all know perfectly well that we did not have one solitary blessed thing to do with the making of this mess over there. And that there is no possible sane and logical reason why we should feel any impulse to take a hand in it.

Did we have anything to do with any promises Britain and France made to Poland? No, we didn't.

Did we have anything to do with Hitler's landgrabbing? No, we didn't.

Did we have anything to do with Britain and France declaring war on Germany? We certainly did not and were not even consulted.

These are some of the SMELLY things in this pit of European back-alley politics into which we will be sucked if we don't watch our step -- if we are fools enough to raise the embargo on the sale of arms to these war-mad European politicians, if we are fools enough to allow ourselves to get all excited about this brawl that is going on over there, as such brawls have, almost since the dawn of history.

Before they started this row over land and natural resources, did they ask our advice or tell us their plans? Ask for our good wishes or even for our opinion?

No, they did not, and we neither advised nor encouraged them, so why should we get all stewed up about it and furnish the ammunition to keep it going.

Just because people on the other side of the world insist on continuing their age-old practise of committing mass suicide, do we as a nation have to follow their example and blow out our brains too.

GENERAL BUTLER - 2.

Are we to adopt a policy of sitting around this European cock-pit and going to the rescue of our favorite cocks whenever they get themselves into a fight they might not be able to win without us?

Are we to become so entangled in European high pressure poli-tics that the main issue at our elections will be whether or not to allow political changes abroad?

If we are to make it our practise to take part in these cock-fights over there we should certainly vote on it - have it in all our national political platforms every time we have an election.

Twenty-five years ago we sold them munitions and then had to go abroad to bail out Britain and France, helped drench the gore-sodden fields of Europe with the blood of a quarter million of our finest boys - the pride of our manhood - helped sow the seeds of the present orgy - spent fifty billion dollars on that venture. Are we to keep on doing it?

Are WE to blame because Hitler built himself a great hair-trigger war machine that crushes everything in front of it?

Are WE responsible that England and France did not build a machine to stop him?

Are WE culpable in any way because Hitler started before the other side was ready?

Provided Britain and France really want to stop Hitler, are WE to make up for their failure to prepare to do so by sticking out OUR necks and raising our embargo on arms? Raise the gates and furnish them the wherewithal to fight? They really don't want mun-itions - are not using what they have - No, they want our man power.

Suppose you are walking down a strange street in a strange town in a strange country thousands of miles from your own home. You come across a brawl. You have no real interest in it. All of a sudden you hear one of the brawlers cry out, in your native tongue, as he swats his opponent: "I believe in Democracy." You don't know in the least what the fight is about but your sympathies at once are with this fellow who speaks your own language. The believer in Democracy sees you hesitate and shouts: "Come on and get in -- we believe in the same things. Also, don't forget, if this other fellow wins, you'll be next. You'd better come in now."

You reply, "No, I don't want to. I'm a stranger and don't want to get mixed up in this. I like you but not enough to get in-to a fight. I want to be neutral."

"All right," he says, "Be neutral, but you gather up all the clubs, stones and brick-bats you can get hold of and sell them to me, I'LL use them on the other fellow."

That's a swell way to be neutral, isn't it.

Do you really think that if you start handing your Democratic friend ammunition, you won't get into it too? You can't help it,

GENERAL BUTLER - 3

if he's losing, and if he wins, he will only call you a scab, say he
could have won by himself anyhow, and declare he owes you nothing.
He will also hate you because you made money out of his necessity.
So both sides will hate you.

On the other hand, if you stay out of this fight, with which
you had nothing to do in the first place, the argument that if the
other fellow wins, he will give you a good beating too, won't apply.
You will have gone on about your own business, instead of butting
into a fight where you did not belong, and, better still, the winner
won't find you right there on hand and ready to be chewed up next.
You will be thousands of miles away and he will have to come after
you.

They say -- well, if the French and British don't lick Hitler,
he will be over here and jump on our necks. He'll be bombing our
women and children and shelling our cities.

Don't let anybody feed you that rot. It doesn't take military
education to figure out what I am going to tell you:

It will take NOT LESS THAN ONE MILLION soldiers to invade the
United States with any hope of success. These million men must come
all at once. They must bring not less than SEVEN TONS OF BAGGAGE
PER MAN. One million men, seven million tons of food, ammunition,
whatnot.

For instance, just ONE item: They must bring four hundred
thousand vehicles alone: tractors, trucks, tanks and the like.
They've got to find room for fifty gallons of gasoline per day for
each vehicle for 270 days - that's nine months' supply. Why there
are not enough ships in the whole world, including our own - and we
certainly wouldn't lend them ours - to carry that kind of expedition.
And remember, these ships have to bring with them enough fuel to get
back with - to make the round trips. We certainly aren't going to
give them fuel over here to go home with. Any dumb cluck can see
that.

But here's some more: They've got to have harbors to lie in;
docks on which to unload their stores. You know you can't stop
twenty-five miles out at sea, drop a fifty ton armored tank overboard and tell it to swim ashore and meet you on Broadway. Remember,
that with all the harbors, docks and ships of England and France at
our disposal in the World War it took us nineteen months to get
1,900,000 men to France. And that though this expedition was headed
for a friendly country and all possible help on the other side was
ours, it took months of preparation after the United States had
actually declared war before it was safe to send the troops over.

You know very well WE aren't going to open our harbors to them,
prepare docks for them and invite them in. New York is the only
big one we have on this coast and to block New York Harbor all you
have to do is to dump two days' garbage in the channel, instead of
hauling it out to sea.

Don't you see, it's all a question of supply - this invading
business. Men and munitions, but chiefly munitions. Seems that

GENERAL BUTLER - 4

munitions always run out before the supply of men is exhausted.

Just figure it out for yourselves: For every man at the front,
you must ship every day of the year from your home depots a thousand
pounds of supplies: food, ammunition, gasoline, clothing, medical
supplies, engineering supplies, spare parts, etc., to say nothing
of replacements of the above. If you have 200,000 men at the front,
you will have 800,000 supplying them from the rear - and you will
have to send them 100,000 tons of supplies every day.

Remember also, that for every thousand miles you go across
water on an invading expedition into a hostile land, you must take
with you ninety days' stores of all kinds. It is over 3,000 miles
across the Atlantic - three times ninety is two hundred and seventy
days - nine months. No, the supply of a European Army in America
is out of the question, that is, an Army big enough to land here.

There is another thing to remember: No fleet can operate more
than 1500 miles from its base and Germany proper would be the base
of a Hitler invading fleet. No he couldn't get his fleet over here,
or get it home again, if he did.

But - they say - he might build a BASE somewhere in South
America. Well, my friends, those who got up that little idea overlooked the fact that it is farther by a good deal from Berlin to
South America than from Berlin to New York, so why invade America
via South America? It doesn't make sense, for when Hitler got to
South America, he would be a good deal farther away from us, than
if he had come straight over from Berlin. So don't let that fright-
en you. It is all pure propaganda and insane to talk of Hitler
invading us. And don't forget too, that we have a Navy of our own
and it's the best in the world too.

Now, what about an aerial invasion? Well, - Colonel Lindbergh
and Eddie Rickenbacher, the two foremost fliers we have, already
have told us it's ridiculous to talk of an invasion by air or to
talk or think about bombing New York from Berlin.

But suppose they do invent a plane that might be able to do it.
That airplane has got to make the round trip too. And without landing. With the fuel with which it started. And even if they build
a plane that will do that, we have enough brains in this country to
make some sort of a machine that will destroy it before it hurts
our women and children.

And don't forget we have an air force of our own, and a fine
one too.

So let's take one thing at a time.

This war's in Europe, it isn't over here. And it won't come
over here unless we invite it. And the best way to invite it is to
raise this embargo and sell bombs and ammunitions. They'll have the
stamp of American makers on them and they'll have the R.S.V.P. that
will bring about that invitation. An invitation to go over there
and join in the mess.

GENERAL BUTLER - 5.

Oh, but the boogey boo is that someone will come over here. Don't be alarmed. No one in Europe can afford to leave home. Why, if Hitler were to leave Germany with a million men to go anywhere, if he ever got back he'd find everybody speaking French or Russian. Those babies would move in on him while he was gone.

No, there isn't a single crazy war dog that can come over here. We can build a defense of our own country that not even a rat, much less a mad dog, could creep through.

Let's be consistent. We cry to high Heaven that we are a God-fearing and peace-loving nation and therefore we don't believe in shooting people, bombing their homes, knocking down their cities with cannon.

And we really ARE a God-fearing and peace-loving people, but certainly it's un-Godly, hypocritical and unmanly of us to say to the British and the French: "Sure, we're against this fellow Hitler, but being God-fearing, WE can't shoot him, WE can't bomb him, but we'll be delighted to see YOU do it, and we'll furnish the guns and the bombs. That is, provided you pay us double what they're worth. And in order that there may be no mistake about it this time, you'll pay us in advance.

You see we're against going to war ourselves, but we're not against YOUR wars. You go ahead. WE'll sell you the stuff."

The majority of the people of this country are against Hitler but don't want to get into this war in Europe.

Our people think the best way to stay out of it is to be neutral.

How is it proposed to stay neutral? Why, by regulating the sale of our products.

It was satisfactorily proved that the sale of munitions to the Allies in 1914-15-16 got us into the World War. Now if we sell it again we run the same risk. If the sale of products has a tendency to involve us, certainly the more we sell, the greater the risk of getting in. The more we sell, the greater the business and the profits, and the greater the profits the greater our interest in the success of our customer.

Our business slogan is: "Our customer is always right." Isn't it?

The present embargo on sale of munitions certainly limits the volume of our sales. It most certainly cuts out blood money. So why raise it - why open the gate and run the greater risk?

Why? To make sure Hitler is licked. But then, we would not be neutral and we have pinned our hopes of staying out on our being neutral. It certainly does not make sense: to raise the embargo and try to stay neutral at the same time.

Also the time has come when we have got to answer another big question before US:

GENERAL BUTLER - 6.

How often are we going over there to bail out Europe? Will we have to do it every twenty-five years?

In addition to going ourselves last time, are we going to send our children today, are we going to be ready to send our grand-children twenty-five years from now?

Isn't it time to make a stand about this thing here and now?

Are we so vitally interested right now that we want to contri-bute five million of the finest and strongest boys that the great Mothers of America have produced? Are you mothers and fathers so deeply concerned that you want to furnish your sons? Well, - start selling them ammunition, and that's what you'll have to do.

Don't you realize that the money you'll get for your ammunition will be covered with blood? And as time goes on, this blood will become the blood of your own children.

Has blood money ever brought anything but misery to those who got that money?

Look what happened to the billions of dollars we made out of the last war! It brought us a situation where even today - twenty years later - there are ten millions of us out of work. And if we allow ourselves to handle any more of this stinking blood money, there'll be twenty millions of us out of work - maybe for the next fifty years.

Also let's look at this question from a personal view point, which is the only one that counts in the long run:

It's all very well and high sounding to say:

The Government declares war.

To say helplessly: As individuals we have nothing to do with it, can't prevent it.

But WHO ARE "WE"?

Well, "WE" right now are the mothers and fathers of every able-bodied boy of military age in the United States. "WE" are also you young men of voting age and over, that they'll use for cannon fodder. And "WE" can prevent it.

Now, - YOU MOTHERS, particularly:

The only way you can resist all this war hysteria and beating tomtoms is by hanging onto the love you bear your boys. When you listen to some well-worded, well-delivered war speech, just remember it's nothing but Sound. It's your boy that matters. And no amount of sound can make up to you for the loss of your boy.

After you've heard one of those speeches and your blood is all hot and you want to go and bite someone like Hitler, - go upstairs where your boy's asleep. Go into his bedroom. You'll find him

GENERAL BUTLER - 7.

lying there, pillows all messed up, covers all tangled, sleeping
away so hard. Look at him. Put your hand on that spot at the back
of his neck, the place you used to love to kiss when he was a baby.
Just stroke it a little. You won't wake him up, he knows it's <u>you</u>.
Just look at his strong fine young body - because only the BEST
boys are chosen for war. Look at this splendid young creature
who's part of yourself. You brought him into the world. You cared
for him. That boy relies on you. You taught him to do that, didn't
you.

Now I ask you: Are you going to run out on him? Are you going
to let someone beat a drum or blow a bugle and make him chase after
it and be killed or crippled in a foreign land? Are the Mothers of
America ashamed to make this fight to stay out of this European War
on the ground of their love for their sons - for what better ground
could there be?

Just realize that you have a fifty-fifty chance of never seeing
your boy again at all, if you let this embargo on arms be raised and
your boy is conscripted and sent overseas to fight. And if you ever
do see him again, fifty times out of a hundred he'll be a helpless
cripple or nervously shot all his life.

Have you ever been in one of those huge Veterans Hospitals it
has been necessary to build to take care of the thousands of helpless and maimed cripples still with us from the LAST war?

If you have, you will not need a reminder of what war can do
to your boy, how it can render his life useless and broken at twenty,
and yet keep him cruelly alive through the whole span of it.

If you have not, I advise you to do and see one of them, for
nothing could bring home to you more clearly or tragically the fact
that in the last analysis it is your boy who is going to pay the
piper. Few there are who come back entirely unscathed, and some
come back in such a way that you would find yourself praying for
their release from pain.

Those withered, elderly, spiritless men who lie and sit so
patiently in their wards day after day in those hospitals, waiting
for the end, as they have waited since they got there twenty years
ago, were the flower of our boys in their time. It is not age that
has brought them to this pass, for their average age is a little
over forty, it is WAR. Like the Unknown Soldier who was one of them,
they too had mothers and fathers who felt towards them as you do
about your boy.

Thank God, this is a democracy, and by your voice and by your
vote you can save your boy. YOU are the bosses of this country -
you mothers, you fathers.

And that brings up another point: if you let this country go
into a European war, you will lose this democracy, don't forget that.

As you stand by your boy in bed, he is safe but here is another
picture. It may help you to build up resistance against all this
propaganda which will almost drown you.

GENERAL BUTLER - 8.

Somewhere in a muddy trench, thousands of miles from you and his home, your boy, the same one that is sleeping so sweetly and safely in his bed with you by his side, is waiting to "go over the top". Just before dawn. Drizzling rain. Dark and dismal. Face caked with mud and tears. So so homesick and longing for you and home. Thinks of you on your knees praying for him. He is frightened to death, but still more scared the boy next him will discover his terror. That's your boy. Stomach as big as an egg, I know, I've had that sensation many times.

Do you want him to be the next Unknown Soldier? The Unknown Soldier had a mother, you know, and a father. He didn't just appear out of the air.

Do you want your boy, tangled in the barbed wire, or struggling for a last gasp of breath in a stinking trench somewhere abroad, do you want him to cry out: "Mother, Father, why did you let them do it?"

Think it over my dear fellow Americans.

Can't we be satisfied with defending our own homes, our own women, our own children? Right here in America?

There are only two reasons why you should ever be asked to give your youngsters. One is defense of our homes. The other is the defense of our Bill of Rights and particularly the right to worship God as we see fit.

Every other reason advanced for the murder of young men is a racket, pure and simple.

It is high time we started to think of Wars in terms of human life, not in terms of money, world position, national prestige.

And yet, if you sit still and allow this thing to happen, if you allow this hysteria to mount, this propaganda to take hold of you, if you allow our national pockets to jingle with blood money, I tell you that you may as well prepare to say good-bye to your boy.

The meat of this whole American Coconut is the Embargo on Arms. Whether or not we run a real risk of becoming involved depends on whether we keep the lid on the Embargo. We know that if we keep it on we shall have no war profits. If we take it off we may make some money, but it will all be "stage money" and covered with blood to boot.

Keep the Arms Embargo on tight! They've been fighting for a thousand years in Europe. Don't let them dot again those blood drenched foreign fields with the bodies of our American boys. Sit down this very minute and write a message to your Congressman, and your Senator, and our President. That's your right - your constitutional right of appeal. It's also your privilege. Right now, I firmly believe it's your duty, if you want to save your boys.

Good night.

ARTICLES

My Services with the Marines
(Undated)

I was born on July 31st, 1881, in the town of West Chester, Pa., and was raised as a Hicksite Quaker, and am still one in good standing as far as I know, and got my first education in the Friends' Graded High School and went to Friends' meeting twice a week, struggling as all the other children did to overcome a desire to sleep through the quiet and peaceful service.

When the MAINE was blown up and the Spanish-American War came on, I was sixteen years old and going to the Haverford School near Philadelphia. Haverford was, and still is, a first class school, but I was not a particularly good student and the only incidents that stand out in my memory of those years at Haverford have to do with baseball, football - and incidents having nothing to do with education. I was a 'day school' pupil and traveled two hours a day on the train - one winter wearing my father's overcoat and carrying my books in the pockets to account for its great size and make it look more natural. I remember our lovable old Latin teacher, not because I learned any Latin from his excellent teaching, but because he could so imitate a storm raging on the sea around the Roman galleys, and we boys took turns asking him to do this for us in order to keep his mind off our lesson, which we did not know. Mr. Wilson, the present head master, was a rookie teacher in those days and we were all very greatly attached to him. However, he had quite an excitable temper, and one day at football practice, I did something he did'nt approve and he shook me so violently I bit off the mouth piece of my nose guard and

swallowed it, causing great consternation on the part of all nearby.
We had a wonderful character as a teacher of elocution, Mr. Knowlton.
He thought he could make an orator out of me and taught me all the
gestures that go with polite speech making and entered me in the yearly
competition, having me learn an oration by William Cullen Bryant. I
did'nt like this, so on the sneak committed to memory Mark Twain's
"Storm on the Erie Canal". On the night of the contest, my mother
dressed me up in my first long trousers and I appeared on the little
platform before all the boys with their parents. Mr. Knowlton sat at
one end of the front row and looked me over approvingly, having
previously assured me that I should win the cup. I can see the dear
old man's astonishment, which rapidly turned to shocked horror, when
I launched forth on Mr. Twain's description of the terrible storm. The
boys, of course, greatly enjoyed this poem, but I did not even receive
honorable mention from the judges, and Mr. Knowlton did'nt speak to
me for sometime thereafter. This, perhaps perverted, sense of humor
has stuck by me all my life and has brought me through every disagreeable
experience I ever had, without an aftermath of bitterness - and has also
frequently gotten me in trouble.

As a football player I was not very good, but I do remember
distinctly a girl giving me a penny before a game for good luck. I wore
the penny in my shoe and rubbed a hole in my heel. On another occasion,
Bill Roper, the famous Princeton football coach, who played on an
opposing team, kicked me in the head and I was out for sometime. This
was the only time I attracted any attention as a football player.

Well, like most other American boys of that age, I was crazy to
go to war, and made an attempt to get into the 6th Pennsylvania

volunteers, a company of which was recruiting in my home town - and also into the United States Navy as an apprentice boy, both of these efforts on my part were blocked by my father who thought I was too young to go at that stage of the war when plenty of older fellows were enlisting. My people were all Quakers and had lived near West Chester for 200 years. Both my grandfathers were Quakers, and both went into the Union army during the Civil War - and both were disciplined for doing so. My father, although a Quaker, did not permit his religious views to interfere with his patriotism, and as a member of the National House of Representatives, voted for this war and had no objection to my taking part, aside from my youth.

On a Friday in April of that year, we played a game of baseball with the Penn-Charter School of Philadelphia and were beaten. I was the Captain of the Haverford team and, although not a catcher, I was selected to do the work behind the bat, as we had a very swift pitcher and none of the other boys had any knowledge whatsoever of catching. At any rate, I was the Captain and it fell my lot to try to hold this boy who afterward became quite famous at Lehigh University.

The result of this game, the first big one my team had played, made me determined to go to war. I had'nt caught very well, and made up my mind baseball was not my strong point. I had behaved very badly toward the umpire, accusing him of cheating, and have always been ashamed of my conduct on that occasion. I have forgotten the umpires name, but hope that, if he should ever read this, he will accept my apology and clear the slate.

Saturday night father came home from Washington, and as I was going to bed, I heard him tell mother in the next room that Congress

had that day increased the Marine Corps by 24 second lieutenants and
2000 men, all for the period of the war. I don't remember that he
said this wise action on the part of Congress made the defeat of Spain
certain, but any real Marine will claim it was a deciding factor. I
remember I did'nt sleep very much, for here was another opportunity
to get into the show. I did'nt know anything about the Marine Corps,
but had once seen a Marine officer with sky blue trousers and red stripes
and liked the uniform. Father further told mother that it was too bad
that I was so young, that I seemed to be determined to go and he thought
highly of the Marine Corps and would'nt mind so much my being in it.

That settled it - and my mind was made up to go as a Marine.

The next morning, I took my mother into the back of the house and
informed her that I was going to be a Marine - that, if she did'nt go with
me and give her permission, I being under the enlistment age and thus
requiring the consent of a parent, I would run away and hire some fellow
to say he was my father and enlist in some far off regiment where I
was'nt known at all. Mother thought it over all day Sunday, and in the
evening agreed to go with me to Washington on the first train to
Washington next day - and without telling father. So, at 4:50 the
following morning, we took the first train from West Chester to
Philadelphia and got a train to Washington which we reached about
10:30. I remember as we rode in the train from Philadelphia to
Washington, my mother frequently reached over and took my hand, and
I recall distinctly how greatly her so doing irritated me - for I was
now a man and did'nt care to have any such demonstration. I have always
hoped that my mother in her great wisdom appreciated the reason for my
lack of affection that morning. I would now hold hands with my mother

in any position or under any circumstance, which simply shows what a
fool a boy is. But, nevertheless, it is only natural, at that age to
pay more regard to outward appearance. You are always far more impressed
with your dignity and with the necessity of creating a favorable
impression through outward appearance as a second lieutenant than ever
afterward in your life.

Immediately upon arrival in Washington, we went to the Headquarters
of the Marine Corps, and while mother waited outside, I went in and
introduced myself to Colonel Commandant Heywood. The old gentleman was
a fine old soldier and was one of the commanding figures of our Corps.
He looked at me and said, "Your father told me you were only 16," I
said, "No sir, that's my brother," and he asked, "How old are you?" and
I said, "I am 18, sir." His fine old eyes twinkled and he replied,
"Well, you're big enough anyhow, and we'll take you."

He sent me across the little parade ground to an old Sergeant
named Hector McDonald, who was in charge of 25 or 30 recruit music boys
and had been designated to conduct an examination to determine the
fitness of young men to enter the Marine Corps.

The Headquarters of the Marine Corps in those days was in the
old Marine Barracks in southeast Washington and together with the
Commandant's house stood within a walled enclosures having been built
in 1800 under the personal supervision of the President of the United
States, which indicated what a busy man the President was in those days.
On one end of the little parade ground stood the big house of the
Commandant, at the other end were storehouses and the band room, in which
the Marine Band practiced. On one side was a little one story building
in which the men lived. In the center was a house known for years as

the Center House, occupied by the commanding officer of the post.
On the other side was a rickety two-story frame building. I remember
the old building well, it had been built by Marines in the beginning
of the 19th century and was not a good job. The doors did'nt fit, nor
did the windows, the stairs were crooked and the whole old building
creaked.

          These old buildings have all been destroyed, and it seems a great
pity as they were so filled with the spirit of our Corps. During the
war of 1812, with Great Britain, the British had occupied these buildings.
Their commander had lived in the Commandant's house and had stabled his
headquarters horses in the barracks. On their evacuating Washington
they had burned these buildings, and by rubbing off the white-wash on
the walls of the bunk houses you could still see the smoke marks. That
old headquarters office building always held great fascination for me,
as so many great soldiers had lived in it. It was on the door of this
building that, according to Marine Corps legend, old General Henderson,
commandant of our Corps for nearly fifty years, had, in 1837, during the
Creole and Seminole wars in Florida, tacked a notice that he had gone to
war with the whole Corps and that headquarters was somewhere in Florida.
He was a rip-snorting old soldier and as in those days there was no
retiring age, continued as Commandant of our Corps until he died at the
ripe old age of 90. He had lived so long in the Commandant's house
that he imagined it to be his own and willed it to his son.

          In one room of these old barracks were the benches on which the
drummer boys learned their trade and I remember the racket was terrible.
However, these old benches had the names of many distinguished men of the
country carved on them, and I recall old McDonald pointing out to me

the initials of John Philip Sousa, who grew up in our Marine Band and became its leader.

When I reported to Sergeant McDonald, I can remember him distinctly, he was tall and sway backed, but one of the fine types you find among the Marines.

He gave me an examination in arithmetic, reading, writing and spelling and after an hour or two pronounced me fit to be a Marine. While we were still passing this examination, I looked out of the window and saw my father rushing wildly across the parade ground toward the Commandant's office and thought my time had come. It is funny, but the mental picture I have of my father at that time is simply that his coat tails were standing out straight, nothing else seems to have permanently registered in my memory. In a few minutes an orderly appeared and said the Commandant wished to see me, and I repaired shakely to his office with its creaky old floor and low, stuffy ceiling. I remember how big and old fashioned the stove looked along the wall, in fact I remember noticing very particularly everything in the room as I stood there waiting for my father and the old Colonel to finish their talk. Eventually, father came across the room and said, "Did thy mother give her permission?" I said, "Yes, Sir." He said, "But thee is under age." I replied, "There is'nt any age limit now, Congress has never fixed one, at any rate, I have attended to that." He said, "How old did thee say thee was?" and I replied, "I told Colonel Heywood I was eighteen, that I was born on the 20th of April 1880." Father looked at me with a twinkle in his eye and said, "All right, if thee is determined to go, thee shall go, but don't add anymore to thy age, thy mother and I were'nt married until 1899." So that bridge was crossed, and I became a Marine.

At that time the Adjutant and Inspector of our Corps was Major George C.Reid, one of the gentlest and finest characters I've ever known. He had a keen sense of humor and was greatly interested in my case. Major Reid had a newphew who entered the Corps at the same time I did and is now a Colonel. The old man took his newphew and me to Heiburgers uniform place and ordered two second lieutenants uniforms, as we could'nt perform our full duties until we were properly garbed. Heiburgers was very busy in those days making uniforms for officers of the Army, so we had to wait two weeks and I remember being greatly disturbed for fear the war would be over before we could get into it. However, eventually, Heiburger finished the job and I had a nice little outfit. I remember it was very tight and I looked very slim and wasp-like. It was covered with braid and I looked very much like a member of a boys' band.

While waiting for these uniforms, father and mother took me to Camp Alger to see our Army which had been assembled there and to witness the big review held by President McKinley. I had no uniform, but was a second lieutenant of Marines and extremely proud of that fact, but a little doubtful as to how a second lieutenant should behave. I had been a member of the Boys' Brigade and had been a corporal, but that was the extent of my military experience and I was not sure how much attention I should receive. We had supper with the Colonel of the 6th Pennsylvania Volunteers and saw the Regimental parade. However, I got into no trouble at Camp Alger due to my rank and returned to Washington that night filled with military ardor and more disturbed than ever that the Spanish would quit before I got a chance at them.

After George Reid and I got our uniforms, we were stationed at
the old barracks in Washington for instruction. It had been the
policy for many years to send young officers there to learn their
profession, and we followed in the footsteps of others. The school
was conducted by the finest old soldier I have ever known, Sergeant
Major Hayes. This wonderful old fellow had been in a Scottish
Regiment and had fought with Kitchner in the Sudan. After his
discharge from the British army, he came to America and became a
Marine. Up to the Spanish American war the Marine Corps had had but
2000 officers and men, and only one sergeant major, Old Hayes, who,
of course, was stationed at the headquarters of the Corps, and to
him was entrusted the bringing up of young officers. The old man
was well along in years, but was a magnificient looking specimen. He
was over 6 foot 3 inches in height and as erect as a ramrod, and must
have weighed 250 pounds. I immediately adopted him as my model.
Major Reid had, to me, a particularly attractive walk and I remember
attempting to imitate him, but, at the same time, I tried to stand
like Old Hayes.

Our schooling consisted in learning the old Drill Regulations
word for word and in drilling in the ranks with the recruits, which
we did several hours a day in the hot sun. There were eight of us
green second lieutenants and Old Hayes held class every morning. I
was by far the youngest and having just come from school could easily
commit to memory my regulations, and to this day I can still repeat
much of them. During the class, the Sergeant Major, being an enlisted
man, always stood up whenever we did in reciting our lessons. You
see, he was an enlisted man and enlisted men never sit in the presence

of officers, and, while he was in charge of us, he could not forget
that there was this difference in our ranks. The old man has been
in his grave many years, but his picture and sterling worth are still
a great inspiration to me. I think, really, he was one of the finest
public servants I have ever known and I have long cherished the
belief that he was genuinely fond of me. I remember on one occasion
I did'nt know my lesson very well and after class he came over to
where I was standing, saluted very punctiliously and said, "If the
lieutenant does'nt study harder, I shall have to restrict him to the
barracks." After this announcement, he again saluted, made a very
military about-face and walked away. You can be sure I studied harder
and did'nt disappoint the old man, and he did'nt have to restrict me.

As student officers, we did Officer of the Day duty from our
front porch. We could see all the sentries and some of us inspected
them by whistling and having them whistle in return to show they were
awake. We used to have dress parades with four companies of eight
men each and the big Marine Band of eighty pieces. However these
first few months of soldiering planted the seed, and I have never
been entirely happy since away from Marines.

Well, after six weeks of this intensive schooling, one afternoon
the Commandant's orderly came over to the barracks and reported that
the Commandant would like to see me. I dashed across the parade
ground and the old Colonel asked if I would like to go to Cuba to the
war, and, of course, I replied in the affirmative. This was about the
first of July and a battalion of 600 Marines had been in Guantanamo,
Cuba, since the 10th of June. They had hit some stiff fighting, and
the papers had been filled with details of their fine conduct, and,

of course, I was very greatly excited and rearing to be off. He
told me that the American Liner ST. PAUL had been chartered by the
Government and was taking the President's own regiment, the 8th Ohio,
to Cuba and would sail from New York the next morning at ten o!clock.
Three of us young second lieutenant were ordered to go, Lieutenant
Reid, Lieutenant Wynne, whose father was later Postmaster General
of the United States, and myself. We had but a very few hours to get
our war outfits together and I remember old Major Reid advising with
us as to what to get. We had no particular uniform shirt in those
days and I bought six stripped affairs for fifty cents a piece and a
little tin trunk. I had six suits of underwear and a sewing bag, an
extra pair of shoes and a Bible given me by my old nurse, and a few
odds and ends. That was my total baggage. Nowadays, you take about
five times as much, however, we were just as happy and gave just as
good service without so much junk.

This was, up to that time, the biggest day in my life and I
remember telegraphing father and mother in West Chester that I was
off to war. The three of us went to New York on the midnight train
and my parents met us in Jersey City, gave us a good breakfast, then
went with us to the ST. PAUL where we reported to Captain Sigsbee,
the former commander of the ill-fated MAINE. Everything was
confusion. We eventually got our clothes stored away in a stateroom
and waited for the ship to move. While I was still in Washington,
homesickness did'nt worry me, but standing on the deck of the ST.
Paul looking at my mother on the dock put an entirely different aspect
on this war business, especially as my father had cheerfully announced
that he thought we would be in Cuba a year. I can remember, very

distinctly, my mother who wore a blue and white silk dress with
large, balloon sleeves, and for months I could close my eyes and see
her on the dock. However, I had done so much talking about this war
that there was no way out of it and I had to go, but was not nearly
as belligerent as I was the afternoon before when our orders first
came.

We finally shoved off that evening and made our way cautiously
down New York harbor to avoid the mines which had been strewn around
to keep the Spanish fleet from coming in.

The trip to Cuba was uneventful. The St. PAUL was a fine old
ship, and while the food was extremely bad and everything was very
greatly mixed up we arrived eventually off Santiago on Sunday
morning, the 10th of July, just one week after the destruction of
the Spanish fleet. We could see the Spanish cruisers lying on the
beach and one of them seemed to be still burning.

The three of us, Reid, Wynne and myself were transferred
about noon that day to the dynamite crusier VESUVIUS, for
transportation to Guantanamo to join a battalion of Marines. The
VESUVIUS was a long, knife-like boat which rocked terribly and got
us all feeling miserable. However, she was fast and we reached
Guantanamo in a few hours.

We went on board Admiral Sampson's flagship, the NEW YORK,
and reported for duty. None of us had ever been aboard a man-of-war
and did'tn know exactly how to behave. We marched stiffly upthe
gang-way in single file and formed in line on the quarter deck,
standing very erectly at attention. We were all dressed up in our
best new blue uniforms and had on our best white gloves and swords,

to say nothing of our high, white stiff collars and patent leather
shoes.

Everybody on the NEW YORK was in working clothes, and as little
of them as regulations would permit, as it was terribly hot. No one p
paid much attention to us for some minutes, however, all the members
of the crew did come back to look us over and we were the subject
of a great deal of comment as we stood staring straight to the front.
Admiral Sampson walked up and down the other side of the deck, and
stopped every once inawhile to gaze at us in an amused way.
Eventually, an orderly brought us our orders and we got in a small
boat and went ashore. The boat landed at a rickety little dock
and we stepped gingerly out in order not to wet our fine clothes.
Some of the 650 Marines were camped near this dock and of these we
asked where Colonel Huntington, who commanded the outfit could be
found. This was our first meeting with this fine body of men,
75% of whom had been in the Marine Corps for periods ranging from
5 to 30 years. The old fellows werepolite enough to us, but we
could see, were highly amused which hurt our dignity very greatly.
They told us that Colonel Huntington's headquarters was on top of
the hill nearby and we started to climb. It was terribly hot and
dusty and we soon lost the spick and span look we had brought ashore.
Reaching the top we found a camp of four or five hundred men inside
some trenches, inquired our way again, and made for the center of
the camp where several dirty looking old men with white beards and
white hair were sitting on boxes. These old fellows had no pretty
uniforms and looked to us to be pretty dirty, and, of course, we
jumped to the conclusion that they were orderlies. I, being the

senior, did the talking and inquired of one the whereabouts of
Colonel Huntington. I can remember the old man very distinctly.
He was short and stockily built with great, big, strong knotty hands,
and prominent nose, with white hair and white beard. The old fellow
was sitting in a home-made canvas chair and looked up at me quizzically
and said, "What do you want with him?" I replied, "We are under orders
to report to him." He then asked if we were going to win the war,
and I informed him that this was no time for joking, that we were
under orders and he would do well to point out the way to Colonel
Huntington. Another old man sitting nearby on a box burst out in a
great roar and fell over backwards; whereupon, Lieutenant Wynne, who
was always of a belligerent nature, spoke up and told him to stand
at attention in the presence of officers. This brought a shriek
of joy from the whole crowd which angered all of us and we were about
to give them a lesson in respect when a private came up and saluted
the little old man in the canvas chair and called him Colonel - and
sure enough he was Colonel Huntington, himself.

    We found that this group of dirty looking men were Colonel
Huntington and several of his officers and the man who had fallen off
the box was my future Company Commander, Captain Goodrell.

    This was a remarkable outfit. Most of the officers of the rank
of Captain or above had been in the Marine Corps during the Civil War
and the junior or baby captain had entered the Marine Corps in 1870.
However, they were a kindly fine lot and received us in a fatherly
way, despite our poor beginning. I was assigned to company 'B' as an
additional second lieutenant and my captain was Goodrell. The old
gentleman had entered the service in 1861 and had a magnificent Civil

War record. He was a strong man and a magnificent character and lived
to be over 90:

Well, old Goodrell took me in tow and put me in a tent outside
the trenches with the remark that I must get ready at once to go
on outpost duty, that our company was going out that night and that I
would have charge of one of the pickets known as the Salt Marsh, as the
regular second lieutenant of the company was sick. He told me to
take off my pretty clothes and gave me some old things to put on.
Before sun down that night we started out. I had charge of about
30 men, and if I live to be 500 years of age, I can never again pass
through such a siege of bewilderment. Here I was, sixteen years of
age, without any training at all and possessing no knowledge of
soldiering, marching out in the bush in the presence of the enemy
in charge of 30 men. I was frightened to death and desperately
dizzy. However I had to go, so stepped out as best I could at the
head of this column. We eventually reached our position to find some
men already there, and my 30 men, without any directions from me, took
their positions and made ready for the night, and it was here I got
my first taste of and love for the fine old enlisted men who composed
our Corps. The sergeant of this detachment was a man named Slater
who had been in the Marine Corps 20 years. He was tall and gaunt and
very hard boiled, but he was a soldier from the ground up and it
did'nt make any difference to him what the President of the United
States sent along in the way of officers, it was his duty to see that
the Marines did well what they were assigned, and he decided that,
despite the handicap of my presence, the Spaniards would not get
throughthat line that night.

I stood around and watched the rest of the men make their preparations. When all was finished, Old Slater came to me and said, "If the Lieutenant would like, I will make his bed for the night." I did'nt. I knew it was no use having a bed, I could'nt go to sleep. But, if Slater said I should go to bed, I was going to bed; so I gave him my little bedding roll and my mosquito net and he fixed me up a little place under a bush and told me I could get in whenever I was ready. I did'nt feel like lying down, all I wanted was to go home to my mother in her blue dress. But as long as I could'nt do that, I preferred to stand up as I did'nt shake as much in that position as I did lying down. About midnight, old man Goodrell came plunging through the brush, put his arm around me and told me I'd be all right, there was'nt much danger of an attack that night and if I wanted anything to come about onehalf a mile through the brush to him. He then told Slater to see that I was well cared for and shoved off to visit the next picket. I tried to think up some excuse to accompany him, but did'nt get away with it and had to stay all night where I was. The mosquitos were terrible and every once inawhile one of the men on duty would let drive at what he would claim was a Spaniard lurking in the bushes. The sudden crack of these rifles completely unnerved me so that by day-light I was a wreck. However, nothing serious happened and about 6:00 in the morning, Slater came over to my bed and told me it was time to get upand go to breakfast, and leaving a few men on duty we trudged back through the underbrush and found the camp just where we had left it the night before.

Every sixth night we had this to do, but as the second lieutenant got well I had no more independent commands and was fortunate enought to be with Captain Goodrell on every other occasion.

The old man was a great soldier and seemed to have no fear whatsoever. I remember on one occasion, after we had taken up our position, he invited me to take a walk in front of the lines and pushed right off telling the sergeant we'd be back in an hour. We walked along the trail about a mile, he pointing out to me the good places for ambushes and giving me a very good lesson in bush soldiering. We saw what we thought were some Spaniards on top of a hill nearby, but this did'nt seem to disturb him at all. He talked to me constantly of his experiences during the Civil War and one night when the moon was bright, he told me that he thought it was a good night for an attack, but not to be alarmed. He apparently saw that I was a little afraid, so went on to tell me some more by saying that every man in the 10th Iowa Regiment during the Civil War had been killed and that he was a bad man to associate with, because all his friends always got shot. However, any luck I've ever had soldiering I attribute to the teachings of this old man, who, according to modern standards, had no military education, but a vast lot of experience which could'nt be gotten from books. When I had the fever he came and read to me and rubbed my hot head and did me innumerable little kindnesses which greatly endeared him to me. I shall never forget the first time he told me to drill the company. I got out in front of it, turned my mind inside out and eventually was able to give some commands which were so conflicting that they tangled the company up and the old man who was sitting nearby told me to get to hell out of there, and said it was'nt worth while trying to straighten the company out and just dismissed it.

We stayed on top of this hill without any action for about three weeks, when we all went on board the transport RESOLUTE and sailed away with our assorted squadrons of tug boats, yachts, etc., for the southern coast of Cuba to take the town called Manzinilo. The RESOLUTE drew too much water to get near this town so we stayed out in the open sea and fired away with our six pounders while the others went in close. Colonel Huntington went over to the flagship NEWArk and came back in the afternoon to say that we would land next morning and capture the town. I remember Captain Goodrell saying that it was a piece of damn foolishness as there were only 600 of us and 6000 Spaniards; that we would all get killed long before we reached the shore. This did'nt make us feel any more comfortable, but we all got ready to go about daybreak the next morning. I had a roommate on the ship who did'nt want to be killed and the prospects of this landing worried him so much that he talked to me all night giving me definite instructions what to do with his valuable pieces of property when he did'nt come back. However, about 4:00 a.m., a little boat came up with a white flag and to our great relief informed us that the war was over, and we did'nt have to go ashore. I don't remember ever having been so greatly relieved before or since and that day we sailed back to Guantanamo to pick up a battalion of artillery of the United States Army which went north with us.

The majority of the crew of this ship were Naval Reserves and were a fine lot, but did'nt know as much about going to sea as they might. I remember one of them telling me what had happened to some

of the crowd earlier in the war. He said some of them had been put
on a old Civil War monitor in the Delaware River and were towed with
the aid of a tug, as the engines would'nt work, and started down the
river to protect the powder works. For some reason the tug had to
leave them for a little while and cast them adrift out in the stream.
The Captain of the monitor was a good fellow, but not entirely familiar
with his job, and did nothing at all when the monitor began to drift
along with the tide. Eventually somebody said to him, "We are going
to bump into some of these boats, if you don't stop this one." And he
in turn stepped up to the bridge of the little monitor and told some
of the crew standing on the deck below to push overboard one of the
anchors. This the crew did, and therewas a splash when the anchor
disappeared in the water. The captain then returned to his cabin
quite satisfied that he had done a good job. A few minutes later
the Executive Officer another good fellow, but not a good sailor,
rushed up and informed him that the anchor which had gone overboard
had not been effective and that the monitor was still drifting around
and around on its way to the sea. The captain became furious, again
took his place on the bridge and gave the order to throw overboard
the one remaining anchor, it having appeared that the first one was
not fastened to the chain and, of course, had had no effect on the
movements of the ship. The executive officer and the willing crew
thereupon shoved over the other anchor, making sure that this one was
fastened to the anchor chain. The anchor splashed in the water and
the anchor chain began to rush out; amid a rain of sparks and great
clouds of dust flew in every direction. The captain was again
satisfied with his job and went below, only to be again disturbed

the executive officer, who said that the chain had'nt stopped and that
the anchor was then about a quarter of a mile up the stream and they
were still drifting. Well, as luck would have it the end of the chain,
which was fully two thousand feet long, was fastened to the bottom of
the ship and eventually the wild career of this monitor came to an end
and she rode safely at anchor.

This all occured when the tide was running out, leaving her in
a position off the oil works at Point Breeze, where a number of oil
tankers were anchored. The tide changed shortly and the old boat
began swooping around on the end of her chain and gathered up several
of these oil tankers and the whole flotilla floated together up the
stream amid the curses of the tankers' skippers, and a request was
made of the Commandant of the Navy Yard at Philadelphia that he remove
this nuisance. I have always greatly enjoyed the story, although I
had great affection for the actors in it and it probably was greatly
exaggerated.

The battalion of artillery which we took on board at Guantanamo
was destined to be our playmates in all the wars which I followed.
Several general officers of the United States Army were among its
lieutenants at the time, the present Chief of Staff of the Army being
one of them. The next year when we went to the Phillipines, this
battalion was on our transport, and they again joined us in the Boxer
Campaign in China, and again during the World War. We left Cuba and
went to Portsmouth, New Hampshire, to a recuperation camp on an island
in the river. By this time I had risen to a position in the company
and was allowed by the other officers to attend all reveille roll call
which meant I got every morning before day light while the rest slept.

However, I greatly enjoyed it and was grateful for even this slight
responsibility. But, I never again was allowed to drill the company
after my display at Guantanamo. The officers and men of this
battalion were a wonderful lot and they have always remained in my
mind as the finest types I have ever known, and I have always been
grateful to them for their patience, as my idea at that time was to
make friends with them by asking great numbers of perfectly useless
questions.

In our recuparation camp we did very little, but rest and try
to keep warm at night. Eventually, in September, I was ordered to
the flagship NEW YORK as the junior Marine officer and was granted a
weeks delay to visit my home. I wore my uniform and tried to stand
up very straight and look soldierly. The men of my company had
cheered me when I left, and I was very happy.

In passing through Philadelphia on my way to West Chester I
had to wait a short time in Broad Street Station for a train. A
woman rushed up to me and asked me what time the next train went
to Harrisburg, and I informed her I did'nt know. She wanted to know
my name and number, and said I was a very poor employee not to know
the train schedules and said she would report me to my superiors and
rushed off. This so alarmed me that I went into the bootblack stand
until time for my train to leave. My week at home was a wonderful
one, and I was received with all the honors of war. The later part of
September I went over to New York and found the flagship in the
Brooklyn Navy Yard.

I knew nothing about life aboard ship, but a fine crowd of wild
youngsters in the "Junior Officers' Quarters" of the ship soon taught

me. The members of that mess who have remained on the active list
are now admirals, and as I see them occasionally it is hard to believe
they once were such carefree boys. At times, they made my life quite
a burden, they locked me in my room until I could repeat, through the
door, the boxing of the compass, and had me do all sorts of ridiculous
things, such as - on one occasion - walk up and down the quarter deck
in the presence of Admiral Sampson carrying an umbrella. On this
occasion the old admiral, who was also on deck wearing a raincoat,
called me over and asked me who told me to carry that umbrella. I
replied that no one had, but that it was raining and I did'nt want
to get wet. The old man laughed and said, "That is the proper answer,
but I know those damn youngsters in the steerage put you up to it."

Early in October 1898, I was sent from the NEW YORK to Philadelphia
to join a regiment of Marines being assembled there for participation
in the 'Peace Jubilee Parade". This regiment was quartered on old
ships lying in the Philadelphia navy yard which in those days was not
much of a place. On the morning of the parade, we went by street car
to the south end of Broad Street, where we formed. Down the street
came the Marine Band from Washington, with my old teacher Sergeant
Major Hayes who had come over to act as Regimental Sergeant Major.
I had been looking forward to seeing Old Hayes again and receiving his
approbation, as I had been in the war and had come home without doing
anything to discredit him. I can remember standing there on South
Broad Street as the band marched toward us, and with it came Old Hayes,
and my heart beat very fast for now was to be my reward. When they were
quite close, I got permission from the captain of my company to go over
and speak to Hayes and I rushed across the street, determined to throw

myself in his arms. But no such thing. Old Hayes drew himself up as
if he had never seen me, saluted in a painfully military manner and I
had actually to reach up to take his hand. I blurted out, "Sergeant
Major, don't you know me?" And he said, "Oh, yes, I know the
Lieutenant." And I said, "Are'nt you glad to see me?" And he said,
"Yes sir, I'm very glad to see the Lieutenant." Well, our meeting
from my stand point fell flat and the whole parade was ruined for me.
Hayes had'nt said one thing to me about what I considered my gallant
service in the presence of the enemy.

We went to Havanna, Cuba, in November and stayed a month during
the last of the Spanish occupation. Havanna was a filthy hole in those
days and not like the present beautiful city. It was crowded with
Spanish soldiers on their way back to Spain, and was altogether a most
undesirable place. However, it was interesting and the visit of a
month passed quickly.

We got back to the United States in time for Christmas. I
remember on the trip down someone said it was time for us to have target
practice in order to use up our allowance of ammunition. So a barrel
was produced, a red flag stuck in the top of it, and the thing thrown
overboard. As we sailed away, those guns which could be brought to
bear were fired and we called it a day.

I stayed on the NEW YORK until all of us temporary officers were
mustered out in the middle of February when I joined my father and
mother in Washington. On the 3rd of March 1899, Congress passed an
Act permanently increasing the Marine Corps to 6000 men and giving us
officers who had served temporarily during the war with Spain an
opportunity to take a competitive examination to receive permanent

commissions. During the month of March, I studied very hard and the
first of April took the examination which lasted seven days, passing
it successfully, and on the 8th of April at 5:00 o'clock in the
afternoon, was sworn in as a regular first lieutenant. The same
time several of us received orders to the Phillipines to take part in
the Phillipine insurrection and we left that night at 9:00 o'clock
for New York to join a battalion of Marines leaving for the Orient.

Dictatorship? (Undated)

Is the United States headed for dictatorship?

Heretofore, the words "dictatorship" and "dictator" have had no definite meaning in our National vocabulary. The words seemed to have a foreign flavor or origin. Their use brought to mind Mussolini and Italy, Stalin and Russia, and, more recently, Hitler and Germany.

Dictatorship is still a hazy subject to us but one that is being widely discussed, almost in an off-hand manner as though a shift from a Democracy of 157 years' standing to a dictatorship involved no more radical change than that of replacing a Republican Lietuenant-Governor of a State by a Democrat.

In the past month I spent considerable time in Milwaukee, Chicago, Pittsburgh, Washington, New York and Newark and in conversations and discussions the question of dictatorship came up.

I wonder how many of the writers and lecturers, and the so-called men in the street who are discussing or advocating a change, know the true meaning of dictatorship?

I wonder if they realize that dictatorship goes hand in hand with constant civil strife, with abridgement of liberty and with bloodshed?

Editor's note: Page two of this document was unavailable and is not included.

and civil strife and bloodshed follow, naturally.

The recent situation in Cuba illustrates a point. Machado was dictator. Elected president, he seized the powers of all the branches of the government and ruled by force, with the backing of his army and navy. But, in all the years of his virtual dictatorship, effort after effort was made to oust him, first by one, then by another group, efforts that were accompanied by riots and killings. Since his hurried and forced departure, Cuba has had a number of governments, and the end, ~~kkkkkkkkkkkk kkk~~ it may be, is not yet. And the people of Cuba are the real sufferers.

In many another tropic land have I seen a dictator rise, seize power by force of arms or some bloodless coup, and, inevitably fall, for no sooner is such a man in power than ~~kkk~~ his enemies begin to plot to overthrow him in order to take over the powers of office.

In all my years in those lands I have known only
of one successful and benevolent Dictatorkkk and in that case
the power was legally vested in him, his rule was over a comparatively small area, with a small population and under special
circumstances.

The benevolent and successful dictator was Major
General George W. Goethals, able, sincere and kindly soldier
who built the Panama Canal. For   years he was the sole
authority, ruling strictly but kindly, over the 150,000 who
comprised the population of the American- directed Canal Zone.

Generally, when dictatorship is advocated, Italy
is pointed to as a shining example of what a Dictator can do.
There is no question that k Mussolini, a remarkable man, has
done a remarkable piece of work in rehabilitating Italy. But
we cannot compare Italy with the United States. Italy, for
years and years, had been at the bottom of the economic heap.

The morale of its people long ago had been shattered. All
hope had been lost. There was no National consciousness. In
the United States we have not approached, even closely, the
low economic level which had been Italy's lot for years. Our
morale is far from shattered.

Our people are liberty-loving; the Italians long
had been used to the rule of the nailed fist which is part of
dictatorship. Our people are undisciplined and not used to reg-
imentation; Italy's were, by training, used to discipline. Italy
is a small, compact, nation, easy to rule by force of arms; ours
is a vast, sprawling land.

Others point to Stalin, in Russia. Again there is
no comparison. The Czars were virtual dictators and the people
became used to being crushed and no matter how harsh the present
dictatorship there may be, it cannot equal that of the Czars.

Still others may point to Hitler. Again, we
cannot compare post-war Germany with the United States. There,
all hope had fled; all other means had failed long ago. Under
the Kaiser, Germany was probably the best disciplined nation in
the world, and her people virtually were unable to move except
as a whole and at a command. Dictatorship comes natural k to
such a people.

Many are prone to speak of a Dictatorship as the
one form of government which enables a nation to meet a crisis
and as a most successful form of government under such circumstances. But we look only at the successful ones, or at the
partly successful ones. What of all the dictators who have
appeared for a brief moment only to disappear in a new revolt?
Dictators whose names were spread across the front pages in
great type for brief periods and whose names are now long forgott

No enlightened nation, (and certainly we may consider ourselves such,) who has had a taste of real democracy and who has inherited a love of liberty as we have, can, or will endure a dictatorship. To many it may seem strange for a military man to denounce dictatorships. For generally, it is the military man who ̶k̶k̶k̶ are advocates of this stern measure.

It is true that ̶h̶a̶k̶ in any military unit the commanding officer is a virtual dictator. In a military force, however, all members of the unit are thoroughly disciplined from the time they join it, and are made to understand that the commander is the sole authority. But in no military unit are there complex̶k̶k̶ problems such as exist in a great nation.

Despite the obvious and numerous objections to a dictatork of the United States, the talk of a dictatorship will gain momentum as long as our economic difficulties remain unsolved.

Many say that the Administration has been armed
with virtual dictatorial powers by Congress. That is stretching
the truth to make a point. Congress has merely permitted the
President certain wide powers to meet a specific and emergency
problem and Congress always has a right to revoke these powers
at its convenience. True dictatorship is the usurping of all
powers of the three branches of our government. That is the kind
of dictatorship that many consider looms ahead for us. That is
the kind of dictatorship which, instead of solving our economic
problems would merely throw our Nation into chaos, as leader after
leader would arise in attempts to wrest the power from the man
in power and set himself up in his place. That is the history of
dictatorships from the day of Rome until today.

Those who see a dictatorship ahead point to the
fact that the present means of disseminating news -- and propoganda
are readily available. The radio is subject to government super-

vision and therefore can be used, as it is now used in Germany,
for instance, solely for government propoganda.

The movies, through the newsreels are easily
controlled in that respect. In America the free press has always stood in the way of a dictatorship. Today, however, many
newspaper publishers feel that the NRA has enabled the government
to censor the press. Under the licensing provisions of the NRA
the government has full power over newspapers and publishers
contend may license them out of business entirely if their news
and editorial comments are not satisfactory to the Administration.

Wherever my experience has been, in Santo Domingo,
in Nicaragua and in Haiti, dictatorships began with press censor-
ship, a kkkkkkkkk from which it was but a short step to the actual
usurping of the press entirely to the state that it became merely
government progoganda organs.

Then commenced the dissolution of Congress, the arrest and jailing of the Supreme Court members and the dictatorship was set up.

The best insurance against Dictatorship is a free and independent press.

The Peace Racket (Undated)

Having devoted most of the years of my life to the study of legalized murder, by which I mean the so-called science of war, I find it impossible to accept the theories of those idealists who are innocent enough to believe that the attainment of world peace is merely a question of joining the World Court, the league of Nations or some other international association for the promotion of brotherly love.

I have said in the past, and I still repeat, that war is a racket. I made this charge long before the Nye Committee of the United States Senate exposed the munitions industry and proved that—for a respectable profit—any manufacturer of armaments will sell his guns to an enemy of his own country. The Nye Committee uncovered some astounding information about the munitions industry, including a confession to profits as high as 800 percent.

But just as the business of war has been an age-old racket, in this country and in Europe, so is the cause of peace becoming a racket. There are at least one hundred or more, known and unknown, national and international, peace societies operating in America and most of them have their headquarters in Washington, D.C. There are probably several hundred minor groups that also believe they are destined to bring about world peace. Many of these are designated by fanciful titles built around the word "peace," while others disguise their aims and purposes with some other name to avoid the charge of being pacifists.

I say the cause of peace is becoming a racket in this country today because every one of these so-called peace committees and organizations must have money with which to function. Salaries have to be paid to executive secretaries and office staffs. Printers must be paid for the publication of pamphlets and brochures. Landlords must have their rent. Lecturers must have expense accounts as well as remuneration. Where are they getting all this money, these millions of dollars that are being spent annually? The answer is simple. We gullible Americans who are philanthropically inclined, dig down in our pockets for generous donations and contributions. We buy memberships on national committees. We are flattered when our names are printed on their stationary, in company with a long list of America's most distinguished philanthropists and world peace advocates. Every penny that these peace societies are spending can come only from the pockets of the American people. Professional pacifists have discovered that they can work upon the emotions of some of our wealthy citizens with encouraging financial results.

I don't mean that all of these organizations are promoted by personal profit seeking individuals. Some of them are headed by sincere but misguided people who have adopted the cause of world peace as a hobby. World peace is a hobby that a lot of people like to indulge because it represents a popular cause, and they enjoy the spotlight of prominence. Naturally, everybody is in favor of world peace. No one who talks or gets emotional about the prospects of world peace is going to afford his neighbor of a different religion, or political creed, or hurt the feelings of a prospective business customer. In fact, the peace racket is harmless hobby in every respect except one. In most instances, the peace racket of today is purely a commercial endeavor that is extracting millions of dollars from soft-headed people by imposing upon their humanitarian impulse with flattery, false hopes and impossible schemes. If these professional pacifists would dare to use the same tactics in nearly any other field of effort, they could be convicted of fraud.

One particular peace seeking group is planned as a thoroughly businesslike, non-profit organization, basing its campaigns on economically sound theories. Its sponsors have apparently accepted the idea that world peace can be accomplished through the education of the masses on the evils of war. They are employing the strategy of a nationwide publicity campaign with full page magazine insertions, outdoor advertising, newspaper columns, radio addresses and the publication of special volumes on war and munitions.

The names of college presidents, editors, authors, professors in theological seminaries, executives of religious organizations and nationally known preachers and rabbis can be found in abundance on stationary that goes out from Washington bearing plaintive appeals for moral support—and frequently for funds. If the funds are not forthcoming in actual cash, the equivalent in free newspaper or magazine space is always acceptable. And when I glance over these names, I think of a little ditty that was popular with a Maryland outfit of negro engineers in the A. E. F., back in 1918. The theme of this little chant was well expressed in the following:

<u>"Oh de states is full o' people tellin' how de war is fit,</u>
<u>But when hit comes to fightin', never fit a single bit."</u>

That pretty well expresses my personal views on the futility of the peace racket. Don't misunderstand me. I am not saying that world peace is an empty dream. I am not predicting that just because we always have had wars in the past, that we must have wars in the future. Once upon a time, in the enthusiasm of my militaristic environment, I really used to think that way. The professional patriots had me, as well as millions of others, convinced that the instinct for war is a human impulse that can never be restrained or refined. Up until my retirement, after more than thirty years active service in the United States Marine Corps . I was absolutely sure that the people of every either country in the world were just a bunch of cut-throats ready to spring Uncle Sam the moment he dared to drop his guard.

But I have learned to think differently, I have spent the past few years meeting and mingling with people all over the country. I have a new conception of the American mind and today I am convinced that we can look forward with some hope to eventual world peace. I admit this condition may not arrive for the next fifty or a hundred years. But in the meantime we can make some headway toward that goal by increasing the normal cycle of years between wars. However, the more I see and learn about the activities of those back of the present peace racket, the more I am convinced that one thing is certain. There is only one element in our American citizenship that can keep us from having another war, at least for the next few generations. That element is composed of the men who stopped the last war. I mean the men who actually did the stopping—the real overseas veterans, the men who went to France and actually lived in the muck and the poison and the blood of war as it was fought on the field of battle, rather than the way it is pictured in history or on the screen.

Don't get me wrong. I am not thinking of the professional veteran—the fellow who spent thirty to sixty days in some nearby camp and then came home posing as one of the "strong, silent men" who helped save the world for democracy. I am not speaking of the chap who by political pull, or through a generous campaign contribution was able to get himself a set of gleaming spurs and the bars of a second lieutenant. Too many of these chaps are active in our veteran organizations today. That explains why in some sections the veteran organizations have thus far failed to reach their peak strength. Too many of these pseudo veterans have taken it upon themselves to speak for the real veteran. And when you hear them on the radio, or the public platform, they will "bleed on the battlefield" more profusely and "pay the supreme sacrifice" more frequently than a thousand other veterans who really know what the hell of war is all about.

The revelations of the Nye committee have demonstrated that the business of making profits out of war is a practical profession. It is not conducted by idealists and visionaries but by men who are politically showed and commercially smart. They use practical methods to gain their ends and they are smart enough to use cold logic in preference to fanciful theories. If that is how people start wars, than that's how we will have to stop them. By being practical, cold and calculating. Most of all, we can be politically intelligent

The overseas veterans of this country are the only ones who can really guarantee the peaceful security of this nation in the future. First, because the overseas veteran is the only man who can speak sincerely and from personal experience on the horrors of war and its futility as a means of setting international disputes. In the second place, the overseas veterans of this country are held together by a common bond of comradeship that can never be dissolved by religious or political differences. This tie of comradeship will always exist between the men who composed the A.E.F. It provides the foundation for an organization nationwide in scope, that can really do something practical in the desire for peace. With the passing of the years, as these men become older, this bond becomes more firmly cemented and the results of their efforts can be preserved.

You ask the question, "How can the overseas veterans of this country constitute a constructive force toward world peace?" Here is my answer. During the years that have elapsed since the World War, the average overseas veteran has acquired many hard knocks, common sense and considerable experience. He represents the one large group of American citizens that is thoroughly disillusioned about the glories of war. He can no longer be fooled by the fanfare and the panoply of marching troops, and the oratorical pap of the flag wavers. In the intervening years since the Armistice, he has had sufficient time to analyze the emotions that drove him forward while in the service. He knows now that he was merely a poem in a game that was being played by others and that all his patriotic emotions were the result of artificial stimulation. Today he recognizes the motive in the propaganda that once nearly made his uniformed breast burst with pride. He realize that most of the people who patted him on the back, when he went away, and told him to "Give the Kaiser hell for me!" never really cared a tinker's darn whether he came back, or how will he might fare should he to lucky enough to return. He has had too many doors slammed in his face when looking for a job. He has heard himself and his buddies, on too many occasions described as "treasury raiders." He has seen too many politicians, and their patrons, benefit from the profits they made cut of the war. He has witnessed too much graft, and waste of government funds, while ready veterans were told by Presidents that they had done nothing to deserve special consideration.

Sad experience has made the overseas veteran practical and that's why these men have reached the very definite conclusion that the only way to stop war is to take the profits out of war. Proof of this trend of thinking in the minds of American's ex-service men was plainly evident when the American Legion held its last convention in Miami. And the veterans of foreign wars of the United States assembled in Louisville. The American Legion took a very decisive step in this direction, with a resolution urging the federal government on the same basis of the wages we pay our troops. In time of war, the veterans want to see the workers in every factory paid proportionately the same as the doughboy in uniform receives. They would let every foremen have a salary equivalent to the salary of a corporal and every superintendent the pay of a lieutenant. Others higher up in the scale of our industrial structure would receive the same money that we pay for the use of brains and intelligence in the Army, Navy and Marine Corps. They are entitled to no more. As far a wealth and properties are concerned, the government should have the same right to take over a building or a manufacturing plant as it has to draft a human

being. As a direct result of this universal draft plan being fostered
and promoted by veterans, I am predicting that legislation of this
character will actually be approved by this or the next session of
Congress.

But these veterans will not be content with merely a war-
time blow at profiteering. They recognize, in the existing methods
and means being employed by the manufacturers of munitions,
a constant menace to the peace and security of America. They
demand that the threat of war be destroyed before it becomes too
late. These veterans ask immediate federal control of all munitions
plants. They would put these wholesalers of death and destruction
out of business without waiting until the belligerents get a chance
to arm themselves for war. They would prevent the promotion
and instigation of wars and choke them off before their incep-
tion. They would stop the sale of arms and arrangements, in this
country, in peace times, to nations that may later declare war upon
the United States and use these same guns to annihilate armies of
American young men.

Among the ex-service men of American we have a group of
citizens whose loyalty and patriotism can never be questioned.
Nobody can accuse them of being pacifists or conscientious ob-
jectors. No one can accuse them of being internationalists. No
one can charge that these men, who have already demonstrated
their respect for American's traditions, will deliver this country
into the hands of its enemies. As leaders of the movement for
world peace, this is the only group of citizens that can hope to
inspire and attract the moral support and the confidence of the
people as a whole.

Unfortunately, the problem of veteran welfare legislation in this country has been a political football from the very beginning. The need to overcome the injustices the truly deserving disabled veteran has suffered, as a result of this situation, has made the ex-service men of this country politically smart. And each succeeding election shows that they are rapidly becoming smarter. To hold their own, they have learned they must resort to the same political tricks, and the same organized pressure, that other groups employ to accomplish their objectives. More than one million veterans are today affiliated with the five major veteran groups. Within the not far distant future, the great majority of America's approximately four and one-half million ex-service men will be banded together as members of these various associations.

Peace will come to this country when we make it impossible for anyone to profit through the promotion of wars. We can never hope to remove the profits of war until Congress passes the necessary legislation. Congress will never adopt such legislation until the individual members of that body are told that they have to vote accordingly or sacrifice their places on the government payroll. The only one who can speak to a politician, and get any degree of attention, is the voter in his home bailiwick. If a sufficient number of these voters make their demands simultaneously. Mr. Congressman will vote to keep his job. After all, the average congress member comes from a district where are no munitions plants and he need not worry about treading on tender toes.

The five major veteran organizations in this country are well organized in every Congressional district. The ex-service men represent the one organized force that can act in this direction.

If those wealthy idealists, and peace loving philanthropists, are sincere in their desires for peace, they will abandon their fancy theories and look these facts source in the face. If they have to give money to the cause—let them spend it in cooperation with the veteran organizations whose individual members will constitute a nationwide force of personal instructors in an educational campaign for peace. By themselves, and with their relatives, veterans can influence the imposing total of at least twenty million votes, and twenty million votes will just about control any election in any man's country. When our peace advocates eventually realize and appreciate the fact that world courts, international leagues and foreign entanglements are merely institutions designed to create further controversies, they will throw these absurd ideas overboard and turn to the who brought our last war to a close to keep us from becoming involved in the next one.

Although this program is fundamentally national in scope, it has a definite relation to the peaceful security of the world as a whole. If the veterans in this country are permitted to demonstrate to the veterans of other countries how they too can lead their people away from the dangers and the havoc of war, the movement is certain to become international. The veterans of France, England and Germany have already proved that they constitute a dominant force within the confines of their own boundaries. They too will be impelled to demand federal control of munitions plants in their respective countries. And when this is accomplished, the people of the world will be closer to universal peace and brotherhood among men than the fondest dreams our most ardent pacifists have ever anticipated.

Let's Quit Kidding Ourselves
(Undated)

A recent newspaper paragraph reveals that statisticians have completed a survey of the mental capabilities of the American people and have come to the discouraging conclusion that one per cent of our population are morons. Based on a population estimate of 120 million individuals, these statistics would indicate we have well over a million morons numbered among our friends and neighbors in the United States. Personally, if this situation exists, I feel certain that this estimate most also include those who are alarmed by statistics cited in support of economic theories. That fairly sums up what I think of statistics and statisticians, and our professional economists who quote statistics to confirm the logic of their conclusions.

Every book, every magazine and every newspaper today offers a variety of causes for the depression and a thousand and one theories that are guaranteed to save the United States from complete collapse economically. The air lanes are loaded with oratorical panaceas and cure-alls. Nine out of every ten people you meet on the street can point out one hundred different weaknesses in our present economic system. At least eight out of these nine are voluble disciples of some different school of thought.

During the past few years I have traveled this country from stem to stem. As a lecturer I have addressed probably several

hundred thousands people, including those who membership in
Rotary Clubs and Chambers of Commerce, as well as those who
might be classed as charter members of the so-called masses. The
majority of my audiences have been composed of former sliders.
This means I have been speaking to a cross-section of America's
citizenship, because when Uncle Sam decided to equip his male
population with uniforms and markets, back in 1917, he took his
recruits from the counting houses, as well as the factories.

In keeping with an insatiable desire to know what the average man's thought are on the popular questions of the day.
I never passed up an opportunity that might help me in my
personal survey of conditions in different sections of the country people everywhere have been grist to my mill--newspaper
publishers, farmers, bank clerks, shop-keepers, cotton growers,
manufacturers, and those who are working as well as those who
are unemployed.

As a result of these interviews, I have reached one definite
conclusion. If one percent of our population are morons, as the
statisticians contend, then the remaining ninety-nine percent of
our people are suffering from an epidemic of delusions that threat-
en to tear down the moral fibre and character of the American
people, unless something happens in the near future in the form
of industrial recovery.

I am not trying to solve an economic situation that is without
parallel in the history of this country. But I am convinced that we
will accomplish little or nothing toward the goal of preventing our
economic difficulties after this depression has been put to rout until the people of this nation decide to face the facts and recognize

truths as they actually exist. Ever since 1929, when we learned to our dismay that there is nothing permanent in prosperity builded upon a synthetic foundation, we have been trying to find some get-rich-quick method of defeating the depression. We have been bombarded with hundreds of different schemes and theories, all of them designed to over-come the evils of hard times without taking into consideration the causes.

Despite all the recovery measures being ballyhooed by the Longs, Coughlins, the General Johnsons, the Townsends and the Liberals and the conservatives, of both the Democratic and Republican parties, I maintain that the major evils that exist today will never be eliminated until the American public regains its common sense and quits kidding itself in anticipation of miracles.

I wear no collegiate cap and gown, and I possess no degrees that might identify me with professional wisdom. I know practically nothing of the scientific theory of economics. My knowledge of the mysteries of monetary manipulations is confined to marine corps pay checks, my monthly domestic bills and household mortgages. In fact, it is the absence of these qualifications and these collegiate degrees that qualify me—in my opinion—to express my views on this particular subject. My vision has not been beclouded by the scientific conclusions of students whose practical experience has been confined to the perusal of ponderous tomes written by students before them.

In 1917, the total gross public debt of the United States was less than 3 billion dollars. The public debt per capita was $28.57. By 1932, the public debt had increased to nearly 20 billion dollars, with the per capita debt increased to $155.85. By the close of the present fiscal year, federal treasury authorities state that our public debt will reach a total of approximately 30 billion dollars. It requires no economic brilliance to understand why taxes are high when our public debt is high – or vice versa.

According to all reports on November 11, 1918, Germany lost the world war. But today the per capita public debt in Germany is only $37.65 while in the United States it is $64.09. It would certainly appear from these figures the report of Germany's defeat was grossly exaggerated.

Before business conditions went hay-wire, back in 1929, our national income amounted to 90 billion dollars. With an income of 90 billion dollars, a tax bill of 10 billion dollars was no serious drain on the pocketbooks of the American people. But when that income is reduced by one-half, and our tax bill jumps to its present status of 15 billion dollars, the circumstances are something to worry about.

Fundamentally, Uncle Sam is merely the head of a household. His problems, on a larger scale, are identical with yours and mine. The moment we, as individuals, permit our expenditures to exceed our incomes, we invite grief. The average man learns from and experience that a beer income is insufficient for champagne tastes. The thrill of "keeping up with the Joneses" can only be temporary, because sooner or later the sheriff or the wolf is waiting at the doorstep. Our politicians and our economic experts may be able to cite a thousand different reasons for our present plight. They can probably likewise suggest a thousand different economic prescriptions. They can point to statistics from here to the moon, and recite theories from now until Doomsday, but unless they recognize that neither Uncle Sam, nor anyone else, can perform the miracle of spending more than he earns—they are wasting their ammunition with a barrage that is landing far beyond far beyond its target.

Obviously, the tremendous burden of taxation required by the federal government is the first result of a deficit in the federal treasury. Heavy taxation, far beyond the tax limits of the average individual income, creates a similar deficit in the bank accounts of the Americans people. If we can reduce taxes to the point where they should be, in proportion to our national income, we will release the brakes on the machine of national recovery and once again the wheels will turn under their own motive power.

Unfortunately, Uncle Sam is hardly in a position to reduce taxes while his overhead expenses are still soaring to the heights. The government must have funds with which to function or it faces bankruptcy. Here is the point I seek to establish. The Americans people themselves are primarily to blame for the bills Uncle Sam is forced to meet today. Back in the days of easy money, we clamored for fine roads, elaborate public buildings, improved harbors, palatial post offices, federal subsidies for the development of aeronautics, and numerous other luxuries that our fancies or whims suggested. Much to our chagrins, we have discovered that these governmental favors and services must be paid for and maintained, even though surpluses become deficits and the national income is reduced by fifty percent. In other words, we, as individual citizens, have ignored the fundamental principle that the piper always wants his pay and that there is only one sure-fire method of keeping out of debt. Pay as you go!

The fad of the moment is to blame congress for all the ills that beset the American people. Congress, as a group, is an abstract body and any orator can direct his shafts at the House of Representatives, or the United States Senate, without much fear of reprisals. Of course, this hardly applies to public officials, because members of congress are naturally resentful of criticism coming from any other individual who is also on the public payroll.

I hold no particular brief for members of Congress, aside from the fact that they are ordinary human begins, endowed with the average amount of intelligence and the same impulses and instincts that motivate the thoughts of the average man or woman. The career of a Congress member after all, is no different than the career of any other business man. Every doctor, lawyer, professional soldier, merchant, farmer, and manufacturer is in reality a business man. Each is engaged in the business of earning a livelihood. Likewise, the art of being a politician is also a business. These men are selling their services as representatives of their constituents. If a majority of a Congress member's constituents demand that he vote favorably on a pending appropriation bill, he can either set accordingly or to be prepared to return to civilian life. There are probably a few members in congress who are situated solely by an unselfish desire to serve the nation as a whole. But the rank and file of these men, most of whom are lawyers, have practically abandoned their private enterprises and have no other major source of income aside from their salaries as either senators or representatives.

In other words, the politician is not the man to blame for our present terrific tax bill. He only favors an appropriation when he feels his supporters demand either his vote or his resignation. Politicians, including the man who hold public office in cities, countries, states—as well as those in congress—have only been doing what they have been forced to do by public sentiment and by the pressure exerted upon them by organized groups of voters. If the politician is guilty of a crime, he is guilty of doing exactly what thousands of others would do if they were in his position. He has been holding on to the only job he has.

There are those who tell us that we can never achieve progress or development—either as a nation or as individuals—until we go into debt. I might agree with this theory, to some extent, but when this debt grows beyond the proportions of reason and sound economics, the theory falls of its own weight. Progress is futile if its benefits are not permanent.

We—the people of American—must come to our sense. This is still the government of Abraham Lincoln's day—of, by and for the people. America must go forward. American will go forward. But let us go forward with the deliberate knowledge that our foothold on the ladder of progress is secure. Let us practice as a nation, the good judgment and sound business principles, that each of us must adhere to as individuals if we wish to avoid financial ruin. We can achieve this through our own efforts if we will stop to remember that we are the ones who must pay the bill and that the luxuries and benefits of progress and development will never be permanently ours until we can pay for them with the cash in hand. Let us desist in our demands for appropriations from public funds until we have surpluses that will pay the costs.

Business and industry can never prosper under the yoke of terminal taxes. Remove this yoke and the people themselves will be freed of the one big burden that creates poverty and unemployment.

We can change, revise and modify our present system of taxation to our heart's content. Personally, I am convinced that certain changes are absolutely essential. I have always held the opinion that those who derive the most from the benefits we enjoy, under our form of government, should contribute the most toward its maintenance. To be specific, I believe in graduated income taxation, inheritance taxes, gift taxes and an adequate levy of taxes on public utilities and those large corporations that would find it impossible to build up such surpluses in any other country. In other words, those who profit the most by government preferment, aid, federal tariffs and protective legislation should contribute the most toward paying the cost of government.

In emergencies, Uncle Sam—as a private individual—should be able to mortgage his holdings or his accumulation of wealth. It is perfectly logical for Uncle Sam to borrow on his financial standing in order to weather the storm of a depression or any other economic crisis. At the same time, even during this borrowing process, Uncle Sam should take steps to pay back the money that is borrowed by tapping the great depositories of accumulated private wealth. We, as individuals, strive to leave this life without passing the burden of family debts to our children. Likewise, I believe that the federal government should conduct its economic affairs in away that will guarantee freedom of debt for the generations to come.

My views on the subject of taxation should not be confused with those of politicians who preach "seek-the-rich" merely as a vote getting slogan. I refuse to abandon the principle that all of us, regardless of how rich or how poor we may be, are indebted to the government itself for certain benefits that all of us enjoy. Therefore, I believe that each should bear his proportionate share of the cost, based on his ability to pay and the size of his purse. And when this country is in the grip of distress, those who possess the greatest surpluses of wealth should be required to contribute the most toward wiping out existing deficits.

However, revision of our tax system will by no means bring a complete solution to America's problem. Our troubles will still be with us if we continue to ignore the basic principles of simple economics. No man has ever acquired prosperity and comfort by spending more than he earns. It is folly for us, as individuals, to think that the federal government can accomplish such feats of magic. Ruinous taxes will continue to be the underlying cause of unemployment, and a constant drain on the resources of business and industry, as long as the people of this country ignore the feat that none of us can ever hope to get something for nothing. We, the people, must foot every bill incurred by Uncle Sam. As long as we forget this obvious feat, and until we modify our demands upon the federal government, and public officials, in keeping with our ability to pay the cost involved, we can hope for nothing but continued distress and painful deficits.

America's Veteran Problem (1936)

Peculiar though it may seem, it has taken us eighteen years to finally discover who won and lost the World War. The Allies may insist they were victorious in the "war-to-end-wars" and point to the Versailles Treaty as proof of Germany's defeat. On the contrary, Germany has ignored the Versailles agreement with an arrogance reminiscent of Hohenzollern ambitions. Under Adolph Hitler, Germany has reconstructed its war machine and today that country is as great a threat to world peace as it was prior to 1914.

In recognition of the stark, brutal truth, we are forced to admit that the World War was a source of profit only to the ammunitions makers while the soldiers—the soldiers of Germany and Austria, as well as the soldiers of England, France and the United States—are the only ones who have suffered losses that can never be repaired.

The men whom we mobilize into armies of robots, artificially imbued with a fierce desire for blood, not only lose out in the economic battle for self-preservation, but they lose step with civilization as a whole, even if they are lucky enough to come back with arms and legs intact. Men whom we train to be killers, in time of war, are never again the same individuals whom we draft from the fields, from the factories or the shops before they become human machines of war.

When war was declared on April 6, 1917, we immediately proceeded to build "murder factories," or cantonments, in all sections of the country. We took boys out of school, young men from behind counters and husky farm lads from the wheat fields, and placed them in the hands of professional soldier instructors in these various assembly plants. During the course of several weeks of rigorous training, we remolded these young Americans. With the tools of severe discipline, strict military supervision, soldier psychology and hate-provoking propaganda, we transformed four million lovable, easy-going American youths into grim-jawed, determined, blood-thirsty killers. They were carefully coached in the use of the bayonet and even told how to grunt and swear as they rushed at a helpless victim. Hard boiled sergeants showed these mild mannered youngsters how to withdrawn a bayonet from the body of a slain enemy with the least possible delay. A hob-nailed boot on the chest of a prostrate body, with a sharp, upward twist, they were told, would do the trick with neatness and dispatch.

With the aid of liberty Bond orators, especially trained war department speakers and specialists in propaganda, we filled the minds of these young men with a loathing for the enemy. By the time they reached the front lines in France, after night long hikes and hungry marches in the rain and of Flanders, they knew the world was mad and they want mad with it. Then came the weary days and nights of scuttling back and forth in rain-filled trenches, sleeping in the slime and the muck of rat-infested dugouts, the constant fear of either a barrage from their own guns, or the guns of the enemy, ceaseless bombardments and deadly gas. Numbed with fright, their ears deafened by the constant roar of big guns, their nerves wrecked by the shock and concussion of exploding shells, these men caught in the cauldron of war, lost their youth almost over night.

Finally, the Armistice brought this havoc to a conclusion. Man had spent his wrath and his strength. Even the professional soldiers who had lived their entire lives as disciples of the war gods were disheartened and soul weary.

We brought these men back to America and shipped them to the cantonments nearest their homes. In less than sixty seconds after they received their final discharge, we again regarded them as civilians. Although they were given intensive training in the art of becoming killers, we gave them no help or training in their readjustment, mentally and psychologically, to the ways of peace. All too abruptly, Uncle Sam gave each of them an honorable discharge and a railroad ticket. We sent them back to their parents, and their loved ones, still dazed and numbed by the horror and chaos of war. There were no orators, no lecturers, no psychologists nor philosophers to help these men understand the transformation that had taken place within themselves, or the changes wrought by the war upon society as a whole. The vast majority of those who made up our armed forces, literacy tests revealed, were mentally incapable of making this diagnosis for themselves. They were young, provincial, unsophisticated and unsuspecting when they were taken from their homes. While they were gone they learned only one thing—the lust for blood.

International bankers may have lost their investments, nations may have lost territories, great military figures may have lost their prestige, and civilians, of both the Allied countries and Germany, may have lost some sleep. But the man who battled with the elements at sea, or crept forward on their stomachs under a hail of bullets, suffered the only irreparable losses that wars create when they sacrificed their bodies, their normal outlook on life and their youth.

Today we have more than a hundred government hospitals filled to capacity with those lads we sent back to civilian life following the Armistice. They are no longer boys in years but of the average age of 45. Mentally and physically, the great majority of them might as well be 60 and 70. Approximately 350,000 World War veterans are receiving help and care from the federal government in the form of compensation for disabilities that have interfered with complete rehabilitation. These men, however, compose only a small percentage of those two million overseas veterans whose shattered bodies and wrecked nervous systems are constant reminders of the experiences they underwent eighteen years ago. In addition to those drawing so-called pensions, there are more than 500,000 World War veterans suffering from disabilities that are either directly or indirectly traceable to their services in the A.E.F. but for whom the federal government has neither a sympathetic care nor a helping hand. This total is augmented as the passing years rob other veterans of their powers of resistance to disease and neurotic ailments.

Immediately following the World War, the federal government discovered it was necessary to adopt certain rules and regulations in dealing with the disability problems of four million veterans. These rules and regulations, embodying certain general principles, have been applied to World War veterans as a whole and without regard to the individual veteran's type or length of service.

In the beginning, Uncle Sam decreed that every veteran entitled to disability compensation would have to prove, beyond a reasonable doubt, through Army records and affidavits, that his disability was directly the result of his service. Officials responsible for these regulations undoubtedly felt the treasury of the United States demanded such safeguards against fraud and deception. To a degree, they were right. Among four million human beings, it is only natural that a certain percentage will possess knavish instincts and cheating impulses. This holds true if these four million human beings are soldiers, bankers, lawyers, farmers, doctors or even ministers of the gospel. Segregate four million people in any section of the United States and you are certain to find a similar percentage of thieves and forgers, murderers and crooks, income tax evaders and grafting public officials.

In applying these strict rules and regulations to a group of men who were suddenly taken from their homes, crowded into the holds of ocean-going ships and reached across the seas to a foreign country, where they were told to kill or be killed, there are certainly some grounds for tolerance and understanding, even at the sacrifice if economy. For about two years, our government naturally showed a desire in this direction. In 1930, Congress enacted a law known as the "Disability Compensation Act." It was created for the aid and assistance of World War veterans unable to provide legal proof and testimony that would convince the federal government their disabilities were actually incurred while in the service. Those who conceived this humane act recognised that the bookkeeping facilities of the A.E.F. were far from perfect, that the A.E.F. was primarily concerned with winning the war and not with the maintenance of records and that the individual veteran was not to be blamed for the inefficiency of former plumbers, or cowboys, or butchers acting as company adjutants or field clerks. They recognized the fact that Companies and Divisions were moved from one point to another under cover of darkness. They recalled that sometimes for days these men were out of touch even with their food kitchens, and their munition supplies, to any nothing of their bookkeeping equipment.

This law also took into consideration the fact that thousands of veterans suffered from hunger and exposure, in the cold and in the rain, in a way that left no immediate marks on their bodies. Any number of front line veterans will testify that they were not always warned of the presence of gas. The poisonous gasses let loose by the Germans had a vicious habit of seeking low places. Many a doughboy suddenly jumped for cover and protection into the pit of a shell hole, only to find it choked with gas, deadly in effect. At times these men caught only a whiff of these vaporous poisons—not enough to overcome them completely or force them to seek first aid. Instead, they sputtered and coughed, and kept on fighting. Many a veteran even refused to confess to a touch of gas for fear his comrades might question his courage, or suspect him of building up an alibi that might take him to safety in the rear. Others feared a trip to a field hospital would mean separation from the payroll and buddies who provided the last human link with what was left of civilization. Every A.E.F. veteran will recall the loneliness and hardships of soldiers who became casuals, attached to strange outfits and perhaps forever separated from their own organized units.

Back in 1917 and 1918, the man of the A.E.F. were healthy, vigorous and in the prime of life. If they came through a skirmish with their limbs in place, they felt sure their stamina would help them overcome the dangers of infection in a slight shrapnel wound or a whiff of gas. They preferred to beg for a dab of iodine, or a couple of C.C. pills, rather than risk losing the companionship of their own comrades.

None of these youths ever suspected that advancing years would weaken resistance powers to shattered nerves or weakened lungs. If they did, it never occurred to them that Uncle Sam would some day say, "There is nothing on your service record to support your claim. We have no legal evidence, and no witnesses, to prove you inhaled this gas, or this growing infection in your leg is an old shrapnel wound."

None of Uncle Sam's doughboys ever thought that he would have to have a group of eye-witnesses to testify they saw him lying for hours in a rain filled shell hole while doing patrol duty; none of Uncle Sam's doughboys, during the bombardment of Verdun, or in the midst of the Argonne slaughter, ever paused to reflect on the necessity of having a personal audience or a camera to observe every act he performed, although the heaviest fighting usually took place in pitch darkness and it was worth a court-martial even to light a cigarette.

The law that took all these facts into consideration, the Disability Compensation Act, lived less than three years. It became effective in 1930 and in 1933, was repealed by the so-called Economy Act, designed to "maintain the credit of the nation." With one stroke of the pen, our lawmakers suddenly decided that 500,000

World War veterans, suffering from disabilities that made it impossible for them to work even if they could find employment, would have to shift for themselves. At that particular time, the country was in the grip of a sudden hysterical demand for economy. In response to this clamor, the politicians decided that political shrewdness required action. They armed the budget up one side and down the other, searching for an expenditure that could be eliminated and still only antagonize that group which represented the smallest organised band of voters. They picked on the veteran.

Despite all the predictions of panic and calamities, the reduction in veteran expenditures was the only major step taken to reduce the costs of the federal government. As soon as this was accomplished, the fad for economy became unpopular and was forgotten by the politicians. On the contrary, they immediately launched upon a spending spree that would put the traditional drunken sailor to shame. For example, we threw 500,000 veterans, each of them disabled physically, into the streets and took away their compensation, ranging from $12 to $40 a month. We turned around and created the Civilian Conservation Corps, with jobs for 300,000 boys and young men, for a flat wage of $30 a month. We repudiated the man who was physically unable to take care of himself, and who had proved by actual service his right to expect a favor from the federal government. We took to our hearts, and to our pocketbooks, the young and physically able individual whose only claim for favorable consideration from Uncle Sam was the fact that he happened to be living within the confines of the United States.

The circumstances that made the Disability Compensation Act both logical and humane were by no means repealed when the law itself was wiped from the statutes. Those same circumstances exist today in even a greater degree. Because of these conditions, the American people may just as well resign themselves to the fact now that sooner or later we must have a general pension act that will provide care and compensation for World War veterans suffering from disabilities that make it impossible for these men to take care of themselves.

This World War veterans pension act is inevitable. Its advent is as certain as the dawn of tomorrow. The politicians who prefer to confine federal expenditures to appropriations that can be divided among their campaign contributors, can howl as they please. The United States Chamber of Commerce, the National Economy League, the Manufacturers Association, the American Liberty League, and the many other groups that are anxious to keep down federal expenditures in order to keep income taxes at a minimum, know that the demand for a World War pension act is on the horizon. Down in their hearts they also know, despite all the opposition they may be able to promote, that a World War pension act will eventually be enacted.

That group of industrial leaders, bankers, and others commonly regarded as representative of "big business," the individuals who compose the memberships of the organizations named above, are fiercely opposed to a World War pension act because the burden of cost naturally be met through taxation. Uncle Sam derives the major portion of his revenue through income taxes. Every step to increase governmental expenses is a threatened increase in income taxes.

Big Business insists the federal government is not responsible for the care and welfare of America's disabled veterans and these men must either care for themselves, or depend upon the charity they can get from relatives, or their local communities. With the hope of protecting themselves against an increase in income taxes, those who oppose the suggestion of a World War pension prefer to discredit the veteran, his sacrifices and the services he rendered to the nation in time of war by castigating him as a "treasury raider" and a "parasite upon the body politic."

When congress eventually enacts a World War pension act, the responsibility of veteran welfare will be placed upon the shoulders of the federal government where it properly belongs. These men were drafted for the protection of the nation as a whole—and not to defend the boundary lines of any particular township, city or state. It therefore becomes the duty of the nation, as a whole, to share the costs of war and the care of its disabled soldiers. This is not only a moral obligation. It is a sound so economic policy that divides the burden of cost between all taxpayers in all sections of the country. It is neither fair, nor equitable, to force any one particular state,and its citizens, to assume the major burden of this expense.

In the eighteen years since the Armistice, World War veterans have moved from one state to another, seeking climatic conditions that are best suited to their health. In the southwest alone, thousands of veterans from other sections of the country have settled to live in the only climate that offers relief from tubercular afflictions.

There is no reason why the taxpaying citizens of Arizona and New Mexico should be forced to assume the responsibility for disabled veterans who have moved to their states from every other part of the country. After having lived for years, and paid taxes, in Pennsylvania or New York, thousands of veterans have moved to other states in search of employment,or for some other reason. The same condition holds true in every corner of the country. As a result, one state may have a large veteran population while a neighboring state may have comparatively few.

There is one inescapable fate in the aftermath of every war. The bill must be paid. It is inevitable that the people themselves must pay that bill. This expense may be met either directly or indirectly through federal state or local taxation or charity. We have not yet reached that stage in America where people are left to die or suffer in the streets. If disabled veterans are unable to get help from the federal government, they will be forced to turn to local agencies. Nevertheless, the people will pay. If these veterans are left to charity, the care of veteran organizations, the American Red Cross, county and state poor farms and hospitals—the burden of cost still rests upon the individual citizen. However, unless this cost is shared by every taxpayer in the country, we saddle the expense upon the shoulders of a few, within the confines of certain countries and states. By dividing this cost between taxpayer's as a whole, the proportionate share of each taxpayer's contribution will be that much smaller. This deduction involves no mysterious arithmetical computations and no complicated theories. The problem is national in scope. The solution is simple. The sooner this fact is accepted by the American people at large, the more quickly will we be able to dispose of our disabled veteran problem and definitely remove it from the field of politics.

Under existing conditions, and even after we have given our disabled veterans the consideration they deserve, the soldiers who took part in the world war will still be the only real losers in that unforgettable conflict between nations.

Government Aid for Veterans (Undated)

Well, if you boys haven't taken the wind out of <u>my</u> sails! I'm telling you—I'm a changed man. "Gimlet-eye!" "Stormy petrel!" <u>Me</u>? Huh—I'm a cooling dove—I'm a woolly lamb that's forgotten how to say baa-a. I'm going around these days with a smile stretched across my face from ear to ear.

Because why? Because you boys are yourselves again, that's why! And is it good to have you back? Why, doggone it, you've got me all sentimental. Just a few months ago I thought you'd all gone forever. I couldn't seem to find a single trace of the boys I used to know. I thought they'd all gone and changed into a lot of dummies standing around with "Kick me" signs pinned to their coat tails. Oh, I heard 'em whining some, and here and there were still a few that stood up and talked like men, but most of 'em were just so many silly geese. They acted like they were out to show they "could take it!" Who wants a soldier who only knows how to "take it!" What does it prove? A straw dummy in bayonet drill can take a lot of punishment, too, so that's nothing to brag about.

But there, I'm not mad. I still get a little hot around the collar when I think of the miseries and injustices and rotten discriminations you have been up against for years—and I haven't forgotten that we've still some distance to travel—but on the whole I'm mighty well pleased with the way you boys have gotten together and backed your enemies up against the ropes.

You see, I'd just about give up all hope. I honestly thought you blessed dim-wits had forgotten how to fight. All I could see was you taking punches—punches on the chin, punches that had you groggy. And that damn near had me delirious! Here I was, going around yelling my head off at you, and thought you didn't even hear me. Congress and Wall Street, and our leading "financial geniuses," whatever they are, and the Economy League and a lot of stuffed shirts who strut on the millions of dollars their crooked old grand-dads sold their souls to the devil to get, were calling you names and kicking you downstairs and blaming you for everything from the price of wheat to the last California earthquake—<u>and you were taking it</u>. First, you let them use you. I don't blame you for that. I've been doing the same thing all my life and I don't know yet how it can be helped.

It's pretty easy to be "against war." Who isn't? Except, of course, the munitions manufacturers and the ghouls who are only too glad to translate human lives and blood and all the other hideous penalties of war into terms of personal profit. But being "against war" doesn't do us much good when war is once declared. It's only a very ignorant person or a fanatic who believes that individual opposition to war, or individual refusal to participate in war, can do away with war. If every man, woman, and child in the United States refused to have anything to do with active participation in war, that still wouldn't affect the <u>causes</u> of war which are international hatred, nation ambition and envy, and racial differences and economic rivalries.

No, the world being what it is, and human nature being what it is, you can't do away with war merely by recognizing war's bitter futility. Once this country is in a state of war, there isn't anything for you and me and every other red-blooded man in the United States to do execept to try our best to make it as short as possible. Secretary of War Dern recently made a fine, intelligent speech in which he said that it isn't the Army that causes war—people cause war and the Army stops it. He's right and only a shallow, superficial, half-naked mind could think otherwise.

But I'm getting away from my subject. I was saying that solders and sailors and marines do the dirtiest and most damgerous jobs in the country when they're called upon. It isn't that we like to kill. We don't really enjoy handling the gun or the bayonet that sends a human soul out into the great unknown, we don't prefer army rations to any other food we ever ate, and most of us have better beds at home than we get in the trenches or in No Man's Land. No—you know and I know—and anyone with a grain of sense should know that men fight wars because there are wars to fight and because, as men, there isn't anything we can do except fight. It's our job. It's any man's job to fight when his country is at war.

But the thing that burns me up is the way govenments and people change once a war is over. Yesterday's heroes become today's blackguards, treasury raiders, snipers behind the lines, and everything else down to and including yellow dogs. A man sacrifices his job, his wife and children, his health and his happiness, and then, when he's down and out, sick, perhaps maimed, if he so much as asks his country to give him enough medicine to keep from dying, enough food to keep from starving, and enough money tob pay for a roof over his head, millions of our "best people"—meaning the richest and stingiest—and bankers and newspaper editors and big income tax-payers, raise their voices to heaven in loud, long yells of protest and rage.

And there was a time not so long ago when you boys actually seemed to be letting them get away with it. They took away your hospital benefits, they took away your disability compensations. They let you go jobless and hungry, they demanded impossible proof of the service connection of your injuries and illnesses, and they blamed you for everything that was wrong anywhere in this whole country. And it seemed to me that you began to actually believe it yourselves. You wouldn't get together. You squabbled among yourselves. You couldn't get far enough away from your own personal viewpoints to see the thing as a whole. You wouldn't coordinate—you couldn't cooperate. You just sat and whined and waited for somebody else to fight your battles for you.

At least, that's how it seemed to me. But glory be, you came to life! For you <u>did</u> get together and you <u>did</u> act and you did get somewhere, didn't you? I've been in and out of Washington quite a lot there last few months. I've been able to watch what your Commander-in-Chief and your legislative committee have been doing. I've followed the militant, unceasing battle that <u>Foreign Serevice</u> has been making for the V.F.W. legislative program and policies. I've been tickled to death with them all but—I'm even more delighted with the way you veteruns have backed up your leaders. You've done what had to be done—you told Congress— told 'em through Jimmy Van Zandt and George Brobeok—told 'em with thousands upon thousands of personal letters and telegrams. Told 'em with your mass meetings, and your veterans' rallies and through the newpapers you've taught to see the light! And it worked!

Congress didn't pass the Independent Offices Appropriation bill over the Presidential veto just because they were tired of being good, obedient little boys. They didn't upset Mr. Roosevelt's nice little apple-cart just to hear the crash. Congress passed that bill because you veterans and your organizations told 'em to—literally. You told 'em why and you told 'em how. You have some good loyal friends in Congress. With their assistance, and the weight of your own united, single-purposed thought and effort, you put over a real concession in veteran legislation.

Every Spanish-American War veteran—every blind World War veteran—every one of those 29,000 totally disabled presumptive cases whose names have been restored to the government pension rolls by the Independent Offices Appropriation bill, have the Veterans of Foreign Wars of the United States to thank for that fact. It's no secret that another veterans' organization, whose name I need not mention because you know it as well as I do, did what the V.F.W. refused to do. They compromised! They went so far as to tell Congress that they were sure the President would sign the bill if it included the compromise measures—75 instead of 100 percent restoration of outs. They must have felt plenty silly when Congress believed 'em and accepted the amendments and then President Roosevelt vetoed it anyway. And they must have felt even sillier when Congress passed that bill over the veto by such a huge majority that it was perfectly evident the bill would have been safe—amendments or no amendments.

At this time of writing, nobody knows what's going to happen to H. R. I, the "bonus" bill. No one can even guess. A lot of editerial writers and other bright boys guessed on the other and they guessed wrong. Lots of people were plenty surprised when H. R. I was passed by 295 to 125 votes in the House. By the time these word are in print, the immediate cash payment of adjusted service certificates may be a closed issue for this Congressional session. It may pass the Senate. If it does, the President's pretty sure to veto it, as you all know. If he does, I think it still has a mighty good chance of being passed over his veto. The first and greatest hurdle it must jump is the Senate vote.

In the meantime, you and I—and every other soldier and veteran in the United States, must keep on working and fighting and pulling together. Even with the Independent Offices Appropriation act, even if the bonus bill passes, we must not forget for one moment that there are still 500,000 sick and disable veterans in this country of ours who have been completely eliminated from the federal pension rolls. We must not forget that these men are just as much the victims of war as the men who lost their lives on the battlefields of France. We must not forget that we—you and I and the V.F.W. and veterans in general—must stand together between those 500,000 men and death—between them and their families and starvation or charity.

Men, this war ain't over yet. I've a mighty strong suspicion that this fight is a permanent fight. We've not only got to keep the veterans' welfare legislation we already have, but we've got to go and get more. We can't stop until every disabled veteran in this United States is being cared for by his country as he ought to be cared for. We can't stop until every heart-broken widow and orphan of a veteran is being given at least a decent living and a chance to live.

If there's anything under heaven that makes me jump up and down and howl with rage, it's the way the United States of America is treating the wives and children of the fine-husky, brave lads and men who died in its honor and defense.

"Thirty dollars a month," we tell these sad-eyed women. "We broke your heart and took away the men you loved and robbed your children of their fathers' love and care, so in return, and by way of cancelling our debt to you and yours, here's $30 a month for yourself and $6 or $8 each for your minor children."

Isn't that big-hearted?

No sir, let me tell you something. As long as there are wars—which means as long as human nature endures; as long as there is human pride and selfishness, and the age-old death-struggle between right and might—just so long will honest, decent, civilized men and women have to fight the forces of greed and power and wealth and man's natural sinfulness.

And just so long will soldiers have to fight their own as well as their country's battles. If there's one thing the last year should have taught us, it is that legislation is never a permanent quantity. Just when it gets to the place where this country is doing the decent, fair, honorable thing by the men whose service and sacrifice have made this country what it is,—a new Congress will convene and start meddling with the statute books. They pick on the laws having to do with government aid for veterans.

The Chip on Uncle Sam's Shoulder
as told to
Barney Yanofsky (Undated)

I f thine eye offend thee, pluck it out, and cast it from thee: it is better for thee to enter into life with one eye, rather than having two eyes to be cast into hell fire.—Matthew xviii, 9.

---o---

I refuse to accept the theory that war is inevitable.

I believe it is stupid to assume that men must fight periodically as an outlet for pent-up hatreds and jealousies. I am not convinced the Creator gives his benign blessing to war as a means of ridding the world of its surplus population.

I find it impossible to agree with militarists who preach the necessity of massive armaments in order to preserve peace. Nor do I have much patience with the pacifist who pretends to believe he can free the world from the scourge of war if people will simply refuse to bear arms under any circumstances.

There are three classes of militarists in America. The first class includes the brass hats in the active military service, These men are naturally anxious to perpetuate their careers in the profession they have chosen. Expansion of the Army, Navy and Marine Corps automatically increases the prospect of promotions. In the regular service, the buck private aspires to the chevrons of a corporal, no corporal is happy until he becomes a srgeant, the sergeant is unhappy until he becomes a commissioned officer; the "second looie" yerns for bars of silver; the first lieutenant craves the double bars of a captain; the captain visualizes himself as a major; the major pines for the status of a colonel, and so on up the ladder of military success and bigger pay envelopes.

The second class of militarists in this country is composed of bankers who specialize in foreign investments, owners of ships that travel the high seas, exporters who make their profits through world trade, the makers of munitions and those who deal in commodities the government always needs in tremendous quantities when it goes to war, such as cotton, oil and wheat. All of these have exclusively selfish objectives in view, and they want Uncle Sam ton have the biggest Army and the biggest Navy in the world to preserve their profits.

The third group of militarists in this country represents honest and sincere patriotic citizens of the type who believe all they are told—without stopping to analyze the motives of the tellers. They are ordinary citizens whose homes are their most cherished possessions. Clever propaganda has convinced these misguided people that the lack of a huge national defense program is a direct threat to their individual homes. These people are convinced an enemy army in apt to swoop down on them any moment, set fire to their homes, murder their children and rape their women if Uncle Sam is unable to send a powerful fleet of battleships to the harbor of Timbuctoo, on the other side of the world.

Just as some people have adopted the custom of shouting for the biggest Army and Navy in the world, as a profession, others have taken up the practice of preaching pacifism as a career. I have no sympsthy with this group because it is content merely with preaching abstract theories that mean less than nothing to the honest soul who wants to work for peaces but doesn't know what to do or how to do it.

Compared to the professional militarist, the ultimate gaol of the sincere pacifist is more praiseworthy and righteous when he pleads wistfully for world peace. My condemnation of the pacifist is confined to those of his kind who make apersonal profit through the dissemination of impractical philosophies that ignore the human element in the causes of war for fear of offending the sources of their contributions. I will never be convinced of the sincerity of these who profess a desire for peace for America, and the world, untill they show gumption enough to go after these goals with the same practical methods a politician adopts to gain his objectives, or a shrewd business man employs in the promotion of his profits.

If America hopes to force the idea of peace down the throats of other peoples, we must first demanstrate we can keep ourselves out of war. The dove of peace may seem to be hovering over the tables of international peaces conferences and discussions. But when diplomats, statesmen and politicians are gathered around those tables you can be sure the dove of peace is only a vulture in disguise.

Every international peace conference that has ever bean held with the purpose of preserving the powerful relations of the major powers of the world has been a complete failure. They have failed because those who participate in these parleys are present only to map guarantees of protection for their mutual possessions and sources of revenue. They are profit-minded and not peace-minded. The subject of peace is only a smoke screen to shield their cagey manuvers in the fields of diplomacy and international intrigue. Their peace pacts have been splendid instruments of harmony—until somebody started a war.

Stripped of all camoufinge, competition for world trade stands out as the cause of nearly every major war in the history of the United States and the world at large.

In the term "world trade" I refer to international financial loans and credits, and the purchase of foreign bonds by investors, as well as the buying and selling of ordinary merchandise and commodities.

Those who framed our Constitution were not unmindful of the profits to be made through trade with other countries. The story of the Colonies discloses that friction with England, the mother country, was first aggravated over the subject of free trade and the right of the Colonists to sell their wares to customers outside the British Empire.

Back in 1775, America was desparately in need of the profits to be made from trading with the East Indies and European countries. In those days the sustenance of the Colonies depended upon our exchange of goods with other countries. Our forebears were still struggling with a wilderness, leasing in machinery and equipment that could produce many of the necessities of life and ordinary comforts.

But even in those days we had prominent citizens who were amassing great fortunes as merchants and ship owner who were profiting from business negatiations abroad. You will find the names of some of these individuals who were engaged in this profitable business affixed to the Declaration of Independence at the time of its adoption.

This was the are in which America adopted the policy that demands "freedom of the seas"—a phrase that was partially responsible for the Revolutionary War, and for every war the United States has had sice them with another country. This "freedom of the seas" policy has been the chip on Uncle Sam's shoulder ever since we found out we could lick even the British Empire if our shores are invaded.

Since 1775, America has witnessed a tremandous rise and fall in its fight for world trade, Recent years have given birth to great strides of progress in other countries. The spread of education and enlightenment, the adoption of modern business methods, machinery and equipment designed to create volume production, has forced America to share its world trade business with other nations. Alarmed by their dependence upon America, these countries have contrived to make themselves nearly independent of commodities they formerly purchased from the United States. Others have adopted American business tricks in order to compete with and undersell Uncle Sam.

The losses the United States has suffered in the field of world trade leave this country today a favorable trade balance of insignificant proportions. In 1937 we are expoting less than 10 percent of all we produce in the United States. In 1929, just before we felt the full effects of the depression, the value of our merchandise exports amounted to more than five billion dollars. In 1934, our merchandise exports dropped in value to hardly more than two billion dollars. In 1954, our merchandise exports dropped in value to hardly more than two billion dollars. In 1929, the value of our imports was approximately four and one-half billion dollars and, three years later, it amounted to about one and one-half billion dollars. Over a period of years our favorable trade balance has not amounted to more than approximately one-half billion dollars annually.

In 1917, when our export business was nearly four times as great as it was in 1910, four years before the World War started in Europe, our exports were worth approximately six billion dollars and our imports nearly three billion dollars.

In 1910, we had a favorable trade balance worth about 279 million dollars, which is indicative of the value of our world trade in years unaffected by war or economic depression.

For the sake of argument, let us assume that three billion dollars worth of world trade was at stake in 1917 when Germany's submarines threatened to throttle America's foreign trade and take possession of the highways of the seven seas for the Fatherland in the event of a German victory.

To save three billion dollars worth of world trade, plus the money invested in European securities, we jumped into a war which experts say to date has cost us at least fifty billion dollars in money alone, to say nothing of the lives that have been ruined or lost.

We will still be paying for the World War for a generation or two to some and the final bill will probably amount to at least 100 billion dollars. All this sacrifice in dollars alone to protect a normal favorable trade balance of not more than one-half billion dollars and our "freedom of the seas" policy.

America must face the cold brutal facts. The people must eventually decide whether or if we want to sacrifice our manhood on the field of battle, and struggle under the load of taxation that is created by wars, merely to save the business enterprises and profits of a handful of our citizens.

World conditions have reached the point that forces America to lock elsewhere for revenues than the loan profits available in world trade. We can no longer hope to compete with countries in the Orient, and in Europe, where people will labor at back-breaking jobs for a mere pittance. Cheap labor costs in Europe, and in the Far East, are making it possible for our competitors in world trade to undersell the American manufacturer and merchant. South America can buy, from Japan or Europe, commodities at a price delivered to its own door step far more cheaply than the American manufacturer can sell these same commodities F.O.B. his own factory.

There is nothing we can do about this situation unless we want to make peasants and slaves of the American working man, unless we want to destroy our high standard of living conditions in the United States, and renounce those principles of social justice we have adopted in order to place the American masses on a comparatively decent living plane.

I am sure this thought is repulsive to the average American. The very suggestion we should reduce our standard of living in this country, in order to bid for world trade on equal terms with our competitors, is repugnant to every clear thinking, fair-minded, patriotic American citizen.

With the realization this change in world trade conditions no longer justifies an international policy that commits us to war if a foreign power, involved in a war with some other country, interferes with our shipping, we should be ready to abandon that relic of the ancient past—our freedom of the seas policy. There is no longer either an economic or on humanitarian reason why this "sacred cow" of American traditions should not be led to the butcher's block.

Here then is the battleground for the militarist who insists he is only interested in preserving the peace and the pacifist who proclaims his desire to spread the doctrine of brotherly love.

The constitution of the United States provides legal methods and means for any changes the people may so fit to make in its intents or purposes.

If the sincere workers for peace will mobilize their forces in every community just as the practical politician does in every precinct, the legislators in every state will be quick to approve the necessary amendment to the Constitution of the United States. When a sufficient number of states approve this amendment to strike the "freedom of the seas" policy from the Constitution of the United States, the United States Congress will act accordingly.

The legislators in the individual state legislatures, and members of the House of Representatives and the United States Senate, will respond to the will of the voters because the voters are their source of bread-and-butter.

Those who honestly crave to keep America at peace must organize their adherents in every Congressional District. They must confine their activities to this one particular objective, untainted and unhampered by partisan politics, and both major political parties will eventually see the handwriting on the wall.

If the preachers, the teachers, the editors and the orators who clamor for world peace will lend their efforts to this movement to keep America at peace, must organize their adherents in every Congressional District. They must confine their activities to this one particular objective, untainted and unhampered by partisan politics, and both major political parties will eventually see the handwriting on the wall.

If the preachers, the teachers, the editors and the orators who clamor for world peace will lend their efforts to this movement to keep America at peace, then the ultimate objective of international harmony is not a vain delusion.

Under this proposed amendment, we can retain our world trade—or what is left of it—without loss in times of pence. If a war should break out between two foreign countries, the private owners of American ships will know they sail the high seas at their own peril.

If they land their ships for the transport of cargoes consigned to one of the belligerents, they will know the loss is exclusively theirs and that Uncle Sam is not obligated to go to war in their defense. We need never deny the sale of our commodities to any country that wants to buy these commodities on the docks of an American seaport. Admittedly, the situation is unfortunate for the small power that lacks adequate shipping facilities. But war and the wholesale slaughter of Americans on the field of battle would be extremely unfortunate for the United States.

The banker or industrialist who still wants to invest his stockholders' money in foreign enterprise can continue to do so. But he will know beforehand that no A.E.F. will be created to protect his overseas investments when war breaks out.

The politician tells us this method of avoiding war will never be effective because the farmer, the cotton grower, the oil field worker and others will raise a storm of protest if denied the opportunity of profiting from high prices for their products in times of war. I grant this situation creates a difficult problem but it is not impossible of solution. The stabilization of marketing condition with steps to eliminate the "lean years" would help stamp out the cry for war-time profits. Moreover, America can consume all that it produces if all of its citizens are granted opportunities for a decent livelihood and the nation's wealth is more fairly distributed among our under-privileged, underfed and underclothed millions.

War is a cancerous infection. Like cancer it can be stamped out if treatment is timely. The doctor who wants to stamp out an infection will first seek the cause of irritation. When the irritation is stopped, the infection itself ceases to spread.

Let us be the first to admit to the world that our greed for profits through world trade is an irritation to war we intend to remove. Let us resolve that henceforth the United States—as a nation—will confine the strength of its military forces strictly to protection against any invasion that threatens America—not merely to preserve the rights of the privileged few who make money in world trade—but the rights and the welfare, the happiness and the homes of all our citizens.

War Is a Racket (Draft)

1. WAR IS A RACKET

2. WHO MAKES THE PROFITS?

3. WHO PAYS THE BILLS?

4. HOW TO SMASH THE RACKET.

5. DISARMAMENT AND DEFENSE.

6. TABULATION OF WAR DEAD AND INJURED
WAR COSTS BY NATIONS
~~COST OF KILLING MEN~~
COST OF WOUNDING MEN
PROFITS MADE IN WAR

Another necessary step is a plebescite before war can be declared. A plebescite -- not of all the voters, but a plebescite of those who would be called upon to do the fighting and the dying. There wouldn't be very much sense in having the 79 year old president of the munitions factory or the flat-footed, cross-eyed head of a garment factory who hoped to gain a uniform contract in war, voting on whether the Nation should go to war or not. They would never be called upon to carry a rifle, to sleep in a trench or to be shot at -- if not shot -- no, only those who would be called upon to risk their lives should have the privilege of voting to decide whether the Nation should go to war. And there is ample precedent for restricting the voting to those effected. Many of our states limit their citizens in the voting. In most, in it necessary to be able to read and write if you wish to vote. In some you must own property. It would become a simple matter each year for the men of military age to register as they did in the draft during the World War, and to be physically examined and those who could pass and who would be called upon in any conscription to bear arms would be eligible

To end or reduce the possibility of war, two general themes have been advanced.

The nationalization of arms and total disarmament.

The Nye Senate investigation into the munitions industries in the U S has as its objective the arousing of public opinion to the extent of the nationalization (in the U S) of munitions and armaments.

While the revelations and sensations developed at these hearings bear out the charge that war is a racket and a mighty profitable one -- the nationalization of arms and munitions will not tend to decrease the possibility of war - at least not to any appreciable extent. The manufacturers of munitions and armaments are not the only ones who find war a profitable racket. As a matter of fact of the $39,000,000,000 that America's participation in the World War cost our citizens only   went to the manufacturers of arms and munitions. The fat profits on the other   that we -- you, and you, and you -- paid for our participation in the war, went to the stock holders, the officers and many of the workers in almost every industry in our land.

Develop figures here.

Disarmament along the lines that disarmament has been practiced since the World War, would not lessen the chance of war -- in fact it would increase it, for disarmament so far, has consisted of what has come to be known as "disarmament by example."

to vote in a National plebescite. They should be the ones to

have the power to decide, and not a Congress, few of whose

members are within the age limit, and fewer still in physical

condition to pass the requirements.   .

          A third step is to make certain that our military

forces are truly forces of defense only.

          The ships of our Navy, for instance, should be spec-

ifically limited to within 200 miles of our coastline. That

is ample, in the opinion of our Naval experts, for defense

purposes. Our Nation cannot start an offensive war if its ships

cannot go further than 200 miles from its coastline. Our planes

might be given a little more territory for purposes of reconnai-

sance, say 500 miles from the coast. The Army should kk never

leave the territorial limits of our Nation.

          Only those who must suffer shall have the right to

vote. No one suffered in the U S to any great extent during

the World War except the soldiers, and of course their immed-

iate kin in the form of worry, etc. Yes, we didn't have as much

sugar as we wanted, although we grew more sugar than ever before

and we had our wheatless days, although we grew more wheat than

ever before and we grew more corn and tye and oats than ever
before, but there was no suffering here. There was enough food
to go around to all the civilians and what happened to all this
surplus food that was grown for the soldiers? And that which
was saved on our various wheatless, sugarless, meatless days?
Why, you say, it was sent to feed the soldiers. Well, it never
got there. Because the soldiers were always hungry. They
lived on half rations all the time. It was that surplus that
piled up in these great warehouses out West and in these granner-
ies during the War years that was one of the causes of the agricultural blight that has encompassed our farms from that day to
this. This surplus/ hung over the farmer like k kh sword of
Damocles and kept prices down and made necessary those numerous
ill-fated agricultural legislations fostered by administration
after administration.

There is no use saying that we can't be pushed into
another war. If we recall kkkkkkkkkkkkkkkk Woodrow Wilson
was re-elected President in 1916 on the platform that he had
kept us out of war and on the implied promise that he would
keep us out of war. Yet, five months later he asked Congress
(and Congress did) to declare war on Germany. The people, in
that five months' period had not been asked whether they had
changed their minds about war. The 4,000,000 young men who
put on uniforms and marched kk or sailed away were not asked
whether they wanted to go forth to suffer and die. What caused
our Government to suddenly change its mind?

The truth is not generally known.

It is known that Lord Balfour, of England, representing
the allied cause visited our shores shortly before that war
declaration and among other things called upon the President,
and a group of advisors Mr. Wilson had summoned to listen to
Mr. Balfour.

Stripped of its diplomatic language, this is what Mr. Balfour told the President and the others:

"There is no use kidding ourselves any longer. The cause of the Allies is lost. We now owe you (American Bankers, American Munition manufacturers, American speculators, American exporters and other war profiteers, five or six billion dollars.

If we lose and without the help of the U S A we must lose, we, England and France and Italy cannot pay this money back — and Germany won't. So...."

Had secrecy been outlawed as far as any war negotiations concerned and had the press been invited to be present at that interview and were the radio then available, the words of this distinguished visitor gone forth to be heard in every home, America would not have entered the war. But this, as most war moves are shrouded in the utmost secrecy, and some polite expression was given by the White House as to the purpose of Lord Balfour's visit.

All secrecy should be eliminated from diplomacy.
Diplomats, as much as anyone else, with their little intrigues
help to foment war. If all the utterances and all the notes
and all the confidences in which the representatives of the
Government partake should be broadcast over the radio, that
cold blooded manner in which lives are staked for dollars would
vanish. And where there are no dollars, there are no wars.

Propoganda is essential to war. ~~Thk~~ It paves the way. By means of propoganda the people are aroused. They are made to feel that war is necessary to their honor, to their security. Capital, while not necessarily controlling the media of propoganda, is able to direct it.

Propoganda, for almost two years, was directed toward

instilling in our people a hatred of Japan.   Why?

Merely because if that hatred could be sufficiently

aroused, we might declare war on Japan. It is easy to see

who was behind the anti-Japanese sentiment in this country.

Those who would profit by such a war. Well, who would profit?

Would it be the young men of our Nation who would leave the

factory and the farm and the schoolhouse and the football field

and the office to shoulder a gun? Would it be their mothers,

their sisters, their sweethearts or their wives? No. It would

be the same crowd. The manufacturers of gun powder, the fashion-

ers of armament, the purveyors of foodstuffs, the makers of

clothing, the owner of metal mines and the various and sundry

capitalists who profit from bloodshed. And why were xxx we asked

to hate the Japanese? On the excuse that Japan invaded China

without a declaration of war, and kill Chinese. Is that any of our concern? Maybe, if we look back in our history we might

find a similar instance. If we recall in 1914, American Marines,

(and I was one of them) and bluejackets were ordered to land

on the shores of a foreign power (Mexico -- the Vera Cruz inci-

dent) fully armed, and there to shoot and kill Mexicans. Kk

There was no declaration of war. Didn't the same administration

order General Pershing and the army to Mexico, still a friendly

nation, to shoot down Mexicans?

So vicious is this war racket that even God is
brought into it.

With few exceptions our clergymen called upon our
soldiers during the World War, to kill the Germans -- that
God was on our side and that it was His Will that the Germans
should be slain, and in Germany, the good pastors there called
upon the Germans to kill the Allies to please the same God,
because God was on their side.

That was a part of the general propoganda, built up
to make our people war conscious and murder conscious. Beautiful ideals were painted for the men who were going out to
die -- as to why they were going out to die. No one mentioned
to them that dollars and cents were the real reason. No one
told them as they marched away that their going and their dying
would mean that the U S steel corporations profits for the war
years would jump from a yearly average of $105,000,000 to $240,000,000

No one told them that the earnings of the DuPont interests (We Won the War DuPonts) would jump from an average of $6,000,000 to $58,000,000; that Bethlehem Steel's earnings would jump from $6,000,000 average to $49,000,000 average. No one told them that the average increase in profits for the four years of the War of those industries directly concerned would increase approximately 300 per cent.

No one told these American soldiers that they might be shot down by bullets made by their own brothers here, or that their ships might be torpedoed by subs   built with U S patents; nor that the barbed wire fences upon which they might become impaled were made here.

They were told that they were going to war to make the world safe for Democracy, and that this was a war to end wars. Well, 17 years after the world has less of democracy than it had then and besides, what business is it of ours whether Russia or Germany or England or France or Italy have democracies or autocracies; whether they are Fascist or Communists. Our problem is to preserve our own democracy.

And very little has been done to make the last war
the war to end all wars.

Yes, we have had disarmament conferences and limitations of arms conferences. They don't mean a thing. We send
our professional soldiers and sailors and our politicians and our
diplomats to these conferences -- and what happens? The professional militariasts don't want to disarm. No Admiral wants
to be without a ship -- no General wants to be without a
command. For both mean men without jobs, and at all these
conferences, lurking in the background are the sinister agents
of those who profit by war. They see to it that khk very little
is accomplished in the way of limitations of arms or total disarmament.

The chief aim of any power at any of these conferences
has been -- not to achieve disarmament in order to prevent war
but to endeavor to get more armaments for the respective powers
and less for any potential foe. There is only one kind of dis-

armament that is practicable, and that is visionary. That is

for all the nations to get together and to scrap ship for ship,

gun for gun, rifle for rifle. Even that would be futile, more

or less. The next major war will not be fought by battleships,

not by the artillery, and not by rifles or machine guns. It

will be fought with deadly chemicals and bases. Secretly, each

Nation is studying and perfecting newer and ghastlier means of

aanhilating its foes. Yes, ships will be built for the ship

builders must make their profits. And guns will be made and

powder and rifles and planes, for the munitions makers and the

plane makers must make their profits, and the soldiers of course,

must wear uniforms for the manufacturers of cloth must also make

their profits and the shoe manufacturers must make theirs --

but victory or defeat will be determined by the skill and the

ingenuity of our scientists.

Even now, witnesses before the Senat's investigation of munitions manufacturers are involved in the sordid
tale of international kkkkk racketeering in arms and munitions of cajolery and bribery, of plots and counterplots, of
secret agreements between the Internation munitions makers,
a story that has kkkk too long been kept from the public.
These disclosures are the frantic efforts of munitions makers
the world over to instil fear into the hearts of Government
that they may buy more and more cannons kkkkkkkkkkkpaik
and more and more powder should lead, as the Senate Committee
hopes it will lead of the munitions industry (This is garbled)

We must not be misled, however, the nationalization
of the arms and munitions industry alone will not greatly tend
to reduce the threat of war. There are still huge profits for
the bankers and the uniform manufacturers and the shoe manufacturers and the mine owners and the food purveyors and all the
other followers whose profits [text unclear].

While the U. S. sinks a $10,000,000 battleship, Japan and England build three new cruisers, each.

35,000,000 pairs shoes, hobnailed service shoes

4,000,000   soldiers   8 pairs each

25,000,000 pairs left over

His regiment had only one pair all during the war

20,000,000 mosquito nets for use of soldiers in France. Never
even taken to France

150 Cavalry and 1,000,000 McClellan saddles

Spent 1,000,000,000 dollars building airplanes that were never
even off the ground   We used foreign ones   Liberty motor p
planes   V 12   Used them after the war but during the war
never had a plane of our own going. Still have thousands of
these Liberty motors on hand. Jenny planes used for training
only but had no combat planes

Undershirts cost 14 cents and sold for 30 cents to 40 cents --
to the Government

4,000,000 sets of equipment stored, knapsacks, etc. that would
have taken a year to use. Are now being scrapped because they
are being changed

40,000,000 yards of mosquito netting to make further nets.
6,000 buckboards, 25,000 sets of harness   144 48" wrenches
Only one nut ever been made that big and that holds turbines at
Niagara Falls. Put on freight cars each one weighing a ton.
Then shunted all around the United States trying to get someone
to use them.

$16,000,000,000 profits made during the war

Not a horse or a mule was used, but they made 6,000 buckboards.
189,000 loaded vehicles to France.

Sold equipment to France on promise of $400,000,000 which they
never paid.

Canned willy.
        investigated   years all
Congress kkkkkkk for two or three kkkk kk special expenditures
of war department. All this was in it. Report of Committee on
War Expenditures.

kk 635,000,000 dollars worth of ships that wouldn't float. Seams
opened up and they sank. Never used any.

100 were lying off Quantico for years.

out of war.

The only way to stop it is by conscription of capital
before conscription of the Nation's manhood.

One month before the government may conscript the
young men of the Nation it must conscript capital.

Let the officers and directors of our armament factories, our gun builders and munitions makers and shipbuilders
all be conscripted -- to get $30.00 a month -- the same wage
as the lads in the trenches get.

Let the workers in these plants get the same wage. All
workers, all executives, all presidents, all directors, all
managers -- everyone in the Nation be restricted to a TOTAL
monthly income not to exceed that paid to the soldier in the
trenches.

Let all these kings and tycoons and masters of industry
and all these workers in industry pay half of their monthly $30.00
wage to their families, and pay insurance and buy Liberty bonds.

Why shouldn't they? They aren't running the risk of
being killed or having their bodies mangled or their minds
shattered. The soldiers run that risk.

Give capital thirty days to think it over and you will
find that by that time there will be no war. That will stop the
racket -- that, and nothing else.

Out of war a few people make huge fortunes. Nations acquire additional territory (which is promptly exploited by the few for their own benefit) and the general public shoulders the bill -- a bill that renders a horrible accounting of newly-placed gravestones, mangled bodies, shattered minds, broken hearts and homes, economic unstability and back-breaking taxation of the many for generations and generations.

For a great many years I have known that war is a racket, but never faced it until I saw the international war clouds gathering again, as they are today. They are choosing sides now. France and Russia meet and agree to stand side by side. Germany and Italy hurry to make a similar agreement.

In the Orient, the maneuvering is more adroit. Back in 1904, when Japan and Russia fought, we kicked our old friends, the Russians, out and backed Japan. Then we were financing Japan. Now the trend is to poison us against the Japanese. What does China's "Open Door" policy mean to us? Our trade with China is about $90,000,000 a year. Or the Philippine Islands? We have spent about $600,000,000 in the Philippines in 35 years and we have private investments there of less than $200,000,000.

To save that China trade of about $90,000,000 or to protect the private investments of less than $200,000,000 in the Philippines, we would be all stirred up to hate Japan and to go to war -- a war that might cost us tens of billions of dollars, hundreds of thousands of the lives of Americans and many more hundreds of thousands of physically maimed and mentally unbalanced young men.

Photo courtesy of the Butler family.

Photo of a young Smedley Butler.

Afterword

By Cindy Sheehan

In 1933, Major General Smedley Darlington Butler, Marine Corps (RET), gave a speech entitled "War Is a Racket." What made this speech so credible, if not surprising, is the fact that Smedley Butler was the highest decorated Marine of all time. Marines today still learn about him, but they aren't taught that he came from Quaker roots and began to castigate the United States and its wars of aggression after his retirement from the Marines.

General Butler is not too well known outside of military/peace circles. Indeed, even though I was a US history major at university and most of what we learned about was war, I don't think I had ever heard of him until about a year after my son was killed in action in Iraq.

In about March 2005, I received an email from a person who had read one of my articles and he sent me a link to the treatise *War Is a Racket*. By the time I first read Butler's work, I didn't need any more convincing that my son Casey died for no reason except profit, but after I read it, I began to understand that the concept of "good war" was a bogus one. Indeed, Butler says this in the first chapter:

> For a great many years, as a soldier, I had a suspicion that war was a racket; not until I retired to civil life did I fully realize it. Now that I see the international war clouds gathering, as they are today, I must face it and speak out.

It seems like every generation, more or less, in the United States we wage a significant war. My generation's "War on Terror" was Vietnam. Smedley Butler wrote *War Is a Racket* between the "good wars," World War I and World War II.

What also makes this treatise so incredible is that in eighty-three years since the original speech, nothing much has changed. If you just change some of the names to the current crop of culprits, it is eerily identical to today.

The poor of our nation kill the poor of other nations, who are unfortunate enough to live in the way of extreme profit. The rich always benefit during war and the poor always pay—always, no exception.

From the treatise:

> Yes, the soldier pays the greater part of the bill. His family pays too. They pay it in the same heart-break that he does. As he suffers, they suffer. At nights, as he lay in the trenches and watched shrapnel burst about him, they lay home in their beds and tossed sleeplessly—his father, his

mother, his wife, his sisters, his brothers, his sons, and his daughters.

My son, Casey Austin Sheehan, SPC US ARMY, paid that terrible price and we, his family, continue to suffer and miss him so much. Hopefully, this book will save lives and prevent more heartbreak.

Take it to heart.

Cindy Sheehan, author/activist
Mother of Spc Casey A. Sheehan, KIA in Iraq 04/04/04
www.CindySheehansSoapbox.com